FOOTNOTES*

FROM THE

WORLD'S GREATEST BOOKSTORES

Bob Eckstein

Foreword by Garrison Keillor

* True Tales and Lost Moments from Book Buyers, Booksellers, and Book Lovers

CLARKSON POTTER/PUBLISHERS

NEW YORK

Copyright © 2016 by Bob Eckstein
Books of Wonder anecdote copyright © 2016 by Mo Willems

Published in the United States by Clarkson Potter/Publishers,
an imprint of the Crown Publishing Group, a division of
Penguin Random House LLC, New York.
www.crownpublishing.com
www.clarksonpotter.com

CLARKSON POTTER is a trademark and POTTER with colophon
is a registered trademark of Penguin Random House LLC.

Library of Congress Cataloging-in-Publication Data
Names: Eckstein, Bob, artist, author.
Title: Footnotes from the world's greatest bookstores / Bob Eckstein;
    Foreword by Garrison Keillor.
Description: First Edition. | New York : Clarkson Potter, 2016.
Identifiers: LCCN 2015045162 | ISBN 9780553459272
Subjects: LCSH: Eckstein, Bob—Themes, motives. | Bookstores in art. |
    Bookstores—Anecdotes.
Classification: LCC NC975.5.E29 A4 2016 | DDC 381/.450020973--
dc23 LC record available at http://lccn.loc.gov/2015045162

ISBN 978-0-553-45927-2
eBook ISBN 978-0-553-45930-2

Printed in China

Book and cover design by Danielle Deschenes
Illustrations by Bob Eckstein
Foreword by Garrison Keillor

10 9 8 7 6 5 4

First Edition

CONTENTS

FOREWORD

When I trotted off to the University of Minnesota back in 1960, three independent bookstores stood near campus in Dinkytown, a stone's throw apart—Perrine's, McCosh's, and Heddan's—each with an owner on the premises, each holding fast to its own sturdy principles. Perrine's stood on an embankment above the railroad tracks, and as you perused the latest fiction hardcovers, you felt the vibrations of the southbound Silver Zephyr heading for Chicago. McCosh's was run by a bearded anarchist who nonetheless loved the classics; he posted incendiary sayings on index cards pinned to the shelves where you could find, reasonably priced, *Ulysses* and *Sister Carrie* and the odes of Horace. Heddan's was run by a silent old Norwegian with a secret filing system—the place was chaos, heaps and piles of books, orange crates for shelves, stacks and mounds and hillocks of everything under the sun, but if you told the old man what you wanted, he'd ponder a moment and go and fetch it.

They were sociable to browsers, of course, and as you became a regular the owner would greet you, maybe mention a book he thought you'd like, and when you left, you'd stand by the counter and discuss the events of the day and feel welcomed and recognized though only a college kid at a big state university—you were a reader, a citizen of the world of ideas.

You become a book lover in childhood because you want to know Important Things and thereby enter the adult world, and the library is your first stop, but you crave ownership, and if you grow up in a family short on money who are careful about turning out lights and mending clothes and buying day-old bread and never eating in cafés, the thought of buying a book is thrilling, a sign of true love. You must have *Walden* in your possession, and Frost and Cummings and Benchley and the great A. J. Liebling and *Roget's Thesaurus* so you can savor all the variations of "to walk," and inevitably you find your way, like an owl looking for a field mouse, like a salmon swimming upstream, like a souse finding a friendly tavern, to a little hole-in-the-wall bookstore patronized by others of your ilk, and there you feel ease and contentment. Nothing against the big chain bookstores, nothing at all, but the feeling is different: like the difference between eating at a café owned by the guy who is cooking and eating from vending machines.

In due course I left the U and wrote a few bestselling books and got enough dough to open my own little bookstore and thereby lose a lot of money in the first five years, but we've hung on and learned a little about managing inventory and now the losses are less, and meanwhile it is a sweet little shop, next door to a bakery, around the corner from a cheese shop and a coffee shop and an Afghan restaurant. There is a big bust of Ralph Waldo Emerson in the front window. Inside, you notice a saying by Flannery O'Connor painted on a column: *Where you come from is gone, where you thought you were going to never was there, and where you are is no good unless you can get away from it.* And farther on, one from Fitzgerald: *Show me a hero and I'll write you a tragedy.* Tables of books, rows of books, piles, a big poetry section, a long wall of fiction, lots of local history, and cheerful women behind the counter and one or two solemn men. There is no sign on the front door, TOILET IS FOR PATRONS ONLY. We only ask that you won't go in the toilet to read—there are couches for that.

The little independent bookstore is dying out, they say. Too bad. Someday mine will, too. The live radio variety show died out when I was a child. The mainstream Christian churches are fading fast, newspapers are getting skinny, the theater is dead (again?), kids today don't know how to use reference books, pop songs don't make sense, tomatoes are tasteless, train travel is on the way out, modern art is hopeless, the celebrities of today are people you never heard of, you can't get a decent egg salad sandwich anywhere, and they don't make movies like they used to. But everything is ripe for revival, I say. Nobody reads poetry anymore and then along come Mary Oliver and Billy Collins. My bookstore is across the street from Macalester College (which is my landlord) and many of our customers are students, and someday one of them will invent a new model for an independent bookstore and I'll be out of business. Perhaps you are that smart person. Good for you.

The real problem with the book business is that smart people have gotten too busy to read. You know it's true. When my bookstore goes under, I will at last have time to pick up a book, sit down, and read it for hour after hour. That's the good life. I'll walk into your bookstore, dear reader, and stand over the fiction table and glance at the wares, read the first paragraphs and the jacket flaps of fifteen novels, pick two, go to the counter, commiserate with you about the sad state of the world, and go home and read. I look forward to that.

Garrison Keillor
AUGUST 2015

INTRODUCTION

Depending on where you are when you read this, independent bookstores are either enjoying a happy resurgence or are still precariously endangered. My first draft of this introduction was all about the struggles of the book business. After all, I'd just spent the past two years talking to bookstore owners and booksellers. I had dates and proclamations from key people, and I went on and on about the plight of bookstores. I couldn't help it—I was entrenched in that dialogue, hearing numerous tearful stories of owners watching their dream being turned into a Foot Locker. But instead of pontificating, I went back to my own rules for this book: keep it brief and keep it interesting.

As far as choosing the bookstores, my selections were based on recommendations, word of mouth, social history, and contributions to the locale. And of course, there had to be a good story from someone I knew or met that was a reliable source. I started with a list of 150 bookstores and eventually narrowed that down to 75. I wasn't able to include all the greatest bookshops, but I do know every bookshop in this book is great.

Bookstores are emotional places both for their patrons and for the employees. They are built on the sweat and tears of hardworking people, each bookshelf lined with the lifework of hundreds of artists. Each of those books represent endless hours of grind and toil. Often the bookstore owner and employees are also writers. Is there a space with more fulfilled or unfulfilled dreams?

The bookstore is also a hangout, a place of solace, a community center, and a venue for cultural entertainment. There are many who absolutely live for bookstores and even those who aspire to live in a bookstore, with some bookstores providing a place to sleep in exchange for work. What other type of store does that? The relationship between bookstores and their customers is give-and-take, reliant on loyalty and generosity. Customers work on the honor system and should be applauded—bookstores can be taken advantage of, dispensing free expertise and human contact only to have their place of business used as a catalog for online shopping, or a library, or simply a restroom. Bookshop owners and employees are a very patient group.

This book is intended to be a celebration of independent stores everywhere and for all those who love books. It was an honor to create this collection of illustrations. While I was unable to include every great shop in this volume—my apologies to those I didn't get to yet— I'd like to think this book is about all bookstores, to all bookstore owners and employees, past and present. This is for anybody who ever dreamed of living in a bookstore.

Bob Eckstein

THE BOOKSTORE

LENOX, MASSACHUSETTS
1966 TO PRESENT

The Bookstore in Lenox, Massachusetts, started in a living room of a small house in an alley behind a café in the neighboring town of Stockbridge. The store moved to Lenox in the late 1960s. Current owner Matthew Tannenbaum worked for the legendary bookseller Frances Steloff and wrote a memoir about it called *My Years at the Gotham Book Mart with Frances Steloff*.

"Filmmaker Stefan Lorant, author of the widely acclaimed *I Was Hitler's Prisoner*, moved here to Lenox in 1940 and lived nearby until his death in 1997. I finally asked him during one of his visits to the store if he knew Hitler personally and what was he like. He stated in an authoritative voice, 'We went with the same girls.'"
—Matthew Tannenbaum, owner

SCRIBNER'S BOOKSTORE

NEW YORK CITY
1913–1989

This Fifth Avenue Beaux-Arts masterpiece landmark building was designed by architect Ernest Flagg specifically for Scribner Bookstore for Charles Scribner's Sons publishing, whose authors included F. Scott Fitzgerald and Thomas Wolfe. The store was forced to move to the more affordable downtown area before it was ultimately purchased by Barnes & Noble, Inc.

"Scribner's top guy had his office above the store. Hemingway was turning in his new novel, For Whom the Bell Tolls, and the C.E.O. was unhappy with a certain word in the manuscript. "What word?" Hem asked. The C.E.O. couldn't bring himself to utter it, so he wrote it down on his desk calendar. Hem agreed to take it out. The following morning, the office secretary wondered why her boss had written, under "Things To Do Today," "Fuck."" —Leon Freilich, "The Poet Laureate of Park Slope"

CITY LIGHTS

SAN FRANCISCO, CALIFORNIA
1953 TO PRESENT

———

For over half a century, City Lights of San Francisco has demonstrated a commitment to preserving the diversity of voices and ideas in literature and promoting literacy.

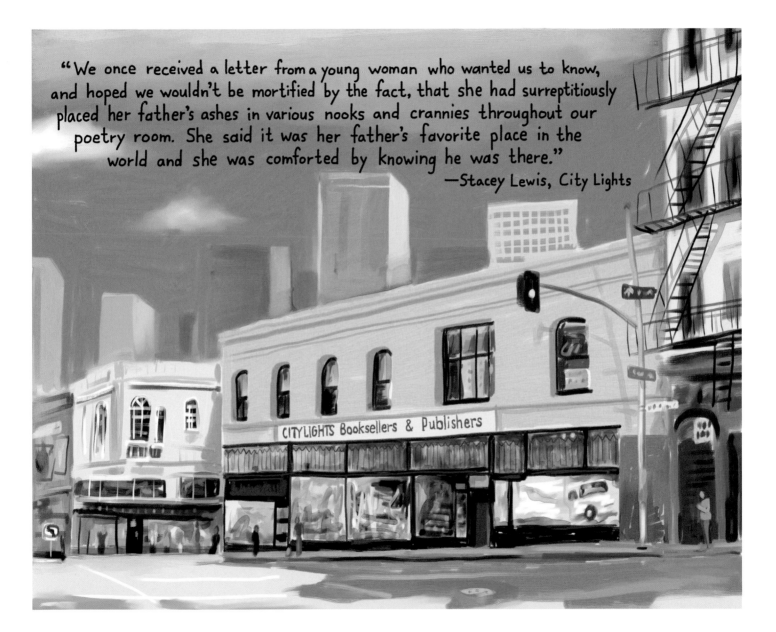

"We once received a letter from a young woman who wanted us to know, and hoped we wouldn't be mortified by the fact, that she had surreptitiously placed her father's ashes in various nooks and crannies throughout our poetry room. She said it was her father's favorite place in the world and she was comforted by knowing he was there."

—Stacey Lewis, City Lights

CITYLIGHTS Booksellers & Publishers

SINGBAL'S BOOK HOUSE

GOA, INDIA
1936 TO PRESENT

Undoubtedly the oldest and the most popular bookstore in the whole of Panaji, Singbal's Book House is a favorite for visitors due not only to its vast amount of travel and tourist books but also a superb selection of national and international magazines and newspapers. In operation since 1936, the shop has also published critically acclaimed art books. The owner of Singbal's Book House, Ajit Singbal, has recently entered the fashion business as well, partnering with the men's apparel brand Indian Terrain Fashions.

Locals boast that Matt Damon walks past this bookstore in the movie *The Bourne Supremacy*, giving this unique five-road intersection 15 seconds of fame.

"It has the look of a book house that at one point in time would have been an important landmark in its own right but is now more of a relic that struggles to find its true mooring in a rapidly changing world." —a local neighbor

THE GOLDEN NOTEBOOK

WOODSTOCK, NEW YORK
1978 TO PRESENT

––––––––––

The Golden Notebook is a popular independent store for local artists and musicians in Woodstock, New York.

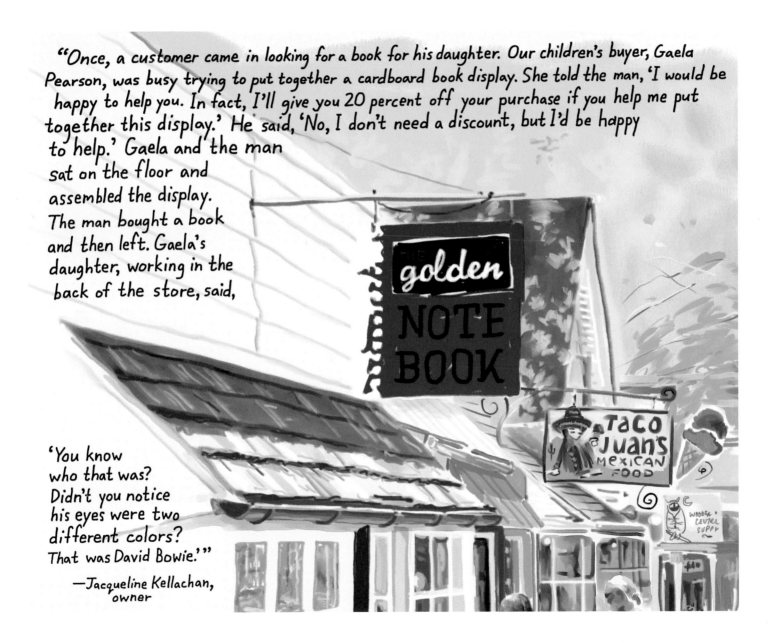

"Once, a customer came in looking for a book for his daughter. Our children's buyer, Gaela Pearson, was busy trying to put together a cardboard book display. She told the man, 'I would be happy to help you. In fact, I'll give you 20 percent off your purchase if you help me put together this display.' He said, 'No, I don't need a discount, but I'd be happy to help.' Gaela and the man sat on the floor and assembled the display. The man bought a book and then left. Gaela's daughter, working in the back of the store, said,

'You know who that was? Didn't you notice his eyes were two different colors? That was David Bowie.'"

—Jacqueline Kellachan, owner

BOOKCOURT

BROOKLYN, NEW YORK
1981–2016

———

Brooklyn's BookCourt was established in 1981. It was voted Best Bookstore in 2012 by the *Village Voice*.

While filming around the corner, Robin Williams came in and looked at the poetry section. "I fucking love poetry! I'll be back." He returned hours later and bought a handful of books. On his way out, he announced, "I fucking love bookstores!"

COMMON GOOD BOOKS

ST. PAUL, MINNESOTA
2006 TO PRESENT

———————

Popular with writers and book lovers alike, Garrison Keillor's Common Good Books is often picked Best in the Cities by *City Pages* and *Minneapolis/St. Paul* magazine. Each year the bookshop conducts an annual poetry contest.

"One Saturday morning, soon after we'd moved to a new, larger location, a customer came in carrying an accordion. Then came another.

Common Good Books

G. Keillor, prop.

Soon we had an entire accordion flash mob. They were joined by a fiddler. We rolled some tables out of the way and celebrated the new storefront with music and dancing. 'Is it always a party here?' asked a customer. 'Yes,' I lied." —David Enyeart, *Common Good Books*

ALABAMA BOOKSMITH

BIRMINGHAM, ALABAMA
1990 TO PRESENT

Alabama Booksmith sells only signed copies, and all books are sold at regular retail prices. Owner Jake Reiss notes that "we have jumped through all sorts of hoops to acquire signed copies from President Jimmy Carter, Tom Brokaw, Philip Roth, Madeleine Albright, Harper Lee, and a few thousand other notables like John Updike, Richard Russo, Isabel Allende, Paul Auster, Pat Conroy, Edna O'Brien, and Anne Rice."

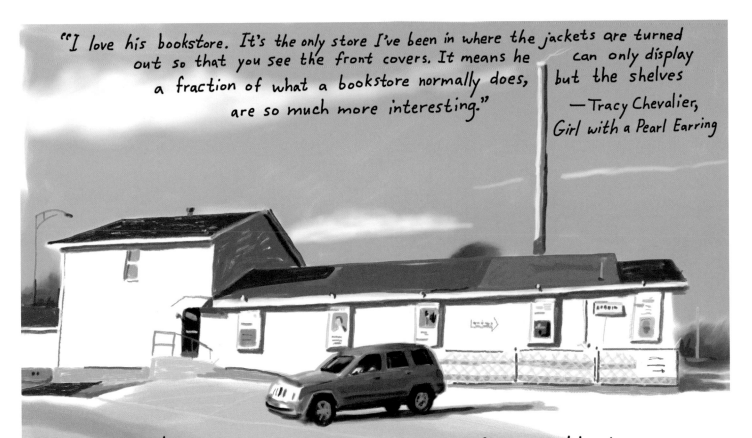

"I love his bookstore. It's the only store I've been in where the jackets are turned out so that you see the front covers. It means he can only display a fraction of what a bookstore normally does, but the shelves are so much more interesting."
—Tracy Chevalier, *Girl with a Pearl Earring*

"Tracy Chevalier was an incredible trooper. Her flight was delayed coming in from Denver and she had not slept in 24 hours. She came straight to the store and signed 400 books for our Signed First Editions Club and then performed in great fashion at a benefit for the Literacy Council. She quickly visited six U.S. stores, then returned to London for Passover to make matzo ball soup." —Jake Reiss, owner

"By the way, the matzo balls turned out like cannon balls." —Tracy Chevalier

bob

KANDA-JIMBOCHO

TOKYO, JAPAN
1877 TO PRESENT

———

Kanda-Jimbocho is "book town" in a small area in central Tokyo; consisting of about 150 bookshops, it is the biggest secondhand book market in the world.

In the late 1860s, schools such as the University of Tokyo, Gakushuin University, Jun-tendo University, Meiji University, and Chuo University all settled in the locale that would eventually house Jimbocho. The first of the area's bookshops—catering to the influx of scholars—opened in 1877. Dozens more followed over the years.

Kanda-Jimbocho has had to
deal with the Great Fire of 1919,
which burned down most of the town; the
Great Kanto Earthquake of 1923, which flattened the
entire area; and then the bombardment of World War II,
which destroyed the shops on the north side of Yasukuni Street
when they were hit by air raids. But bookshop owners say that
their biggest challenge is that today's youngsters are not interested in books unless they are manga.
Most secondhand bookstores in the Jimbocho area face north because shop owners don't
    want their books to be exposed to the sunshine and then fade.

RIZZOLI BOOKSTORE

NEW YORK CITY
1964 TO PRESENT

In 1985 Rizzoli dodged a wrecking ball at the eleventh hour by being designated a landmark. The century-plus-old iconic building wasn't as lucky the second time the wrecking ball reared its ugly head, in 2014. The Fifty-Seventh Street Rizzoli Bookstore in Midtown Manhattan closed in 2014 after being open for fifty years. It reopened in the spring of 2015 in New York City's NoMad neighborhood.

When Umberto Eco lit his first cigarette we tried to tell him he couldn't smoke but he completely ignored us and smoked through-out his signing. He could speak English but chose to speak only in Italian.

"Greta Garbo would spend hours exploring Rizzoli's gorgeous books. Nobody but us knew she was there."
—Antonio Ximenez, painter and Rizzoli clerk, as told by author C. M. Rubin

COMMONWEALTH BOOKS

BOSTON, MASSACHUSETTS
1959 TO PRESENT

Commonwealth Books is located on the oldest street in Boston (Spring Lane, which dates back to 1630), and the bookshop's next-door neighbors include the city's first spring (The Great Spring) and Mary Chilton's home. Chilton was the only Mayflower passenger to settle in Boston.

Commonwealth boasts some extraordinarily rare books and literary objects among its collection, including a 16th-century painting of Chaucer, which is said to be "the oldest not in institutional hands" and supposedly hung in the Chaucer house after his death.
The shop once sold a rare original binding 1508 *Aldine Adagiorum* by Erasmus, considered to be one of the most important books ever by fine-book collectors.
"Erasmus worked at the press as he was revising this work, so it is likely to have actually been held by Erasmus. We hated to see it go," said owner Joe Philips. Erasmus editions only come up for auction about once every 20 years. Commonwealth's copy sold for $70,000.

EL ATENEO GRAND SPLENDID

BUENOS AIRES, ARGENTINA
2000 TO PRESENT

Over a million people each year come to the El Ateneo Grand Splendid bookstore housed in the 1919 Teatro Grand Splendid. It was once the home of a radio station founded in 1924, recording the day's great tango singers and conducting tango competitions. In the late twenties, the building expanded into a cinema, and in 1929 it showed the first talkies in Argentina. The theater is still intact except that the seats were removed in 2000 to turn it into arguably one of the world's most beautiful bookshops.

The stage of the old theater now houses a café, and customers can take their books into the vintage opera boxes to read and relax.

BURKE'S BOOK STORE

MEMPHIS, TENNESSEE
1875 TO PRESENT

———

This Memphis, Tennessee, shop's résumé of famous patrons and visitors includes John Grisham, Richard Ford, Ann Beattie, Anne Rice, Bobbie Ann Mason, Kaye Gibbons, Peter Guralnick, Peter Carey, Lee Smith, Ralph Abernathy, Rick Barthelme, Charles Baxter, Robert Olen Butler, Bill Wyman, Michael Jackson, Lisa Marie Presley, Courtney Love, Gene Hackman, Mary Louise Parker, Benicio Del Toro, Adrian Belew, Carla Thomas, R.E.M., and Matt Dillon. The store celebrated its 140th anniversary in 2015.

Current owners, Corey and Cheryl Mesler, met at Burke's. Corey was manager and saw Cheryl, a student at the University of Mississippi, at the counter buying *Selected Poems of Leonard Cohen*. He elbowed his way over so that he could wait on her and blurted out, "You're buying Leonard Cohen! Will you marry me?" A year later Cheryl was hired at the store.

Cheryl reminisces, "We started dating two weeks after I was hired. We kept it a secret for six months from the owner who forbade employee relationships. She eventually figured it out." Two years after that they were married. The reception was in the store.

They eventually purchased the store outright and have spent the last twenty-five years together in Burke's.

STRAND BOOK STORE

NEW YORK CITY
1927 TO PRESENT

Strand Book Store, legendary home of eighteen miles of books, has been open since 1927, the last standing store of "Book Row," which dates back to 1890.

Many book lovers have had their weddings at the Strand. Someone even once proposed to his girlfriend by placing clues throughout the store as a scavenger hunt, utilizing its famously dark mysterious depths.

"My first job after college was working at the Strand, assigned to the basement. I lasted one week. The day before I was canned, Warren Beatty and Diane Keaton came into the store, looking to shoot a scene for *Reds*. I immediately forgot all about my job and ran up to say hello. All I could think of saying was, 'Could you sign my orange juice?' I got a great Diane Keaton laugh out of her. Maybe that moment of heaven was worth that week in hell." —Alan Steinfeld, producer and host of the television show *New Realities*

QUIMBY'S

CHICAGO, ILLINOIS
1991 TO PRESENT

———

Unofficial flagship store for the graphic novel world. The first section in Quimby's is called Gay Smut. It has a vintage photo booth and a Drugs & Beer section opposite the Children's section.

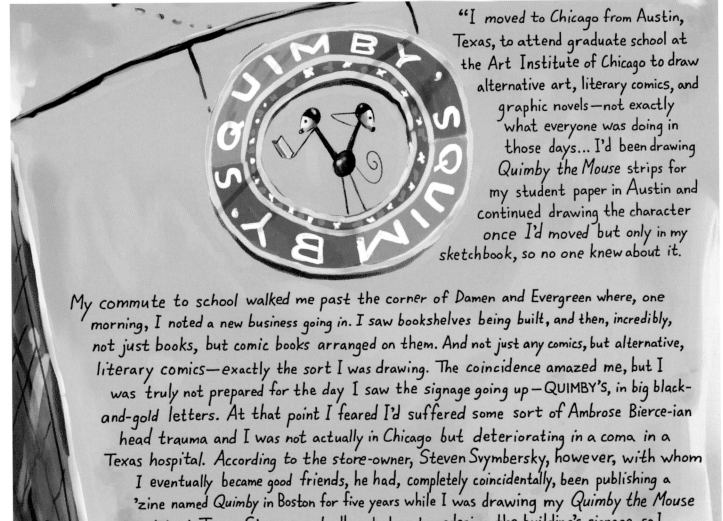

"I moved to Chicago from Austin, Texas, to attend graduate school at the Art Institute of Chicago to draw alternative art, literary comics, and graphic novels—not exactly what everyone was doing in those days... I'd been drawing *Quimby the Mouse* strips for my student paper in Austin and continued drawing the character once I'd moved but only in my sketchbook, so no one knew about it.

My commute to school walked me past the corner of Damen and Evergreen where, one morning, I noted a new business going in. I saw bookshelves being built, and then, incredibly, not just books, but comic books arranged on them. And not just any comics, but alternative, literary comics—exactly the sort I was drawing. The coincidence amazed me, but I was truly not prepared for the day I saw the signage going up—QUIMBY'S, in big black-and-gold letters. At that point I feared I'd suffered some sort of Ambrose Bierce-ian head trauma and I was not actually in Chicago but deteriorating in a coma in a Texas hospital. According to the store-owner, Steven Svymbersky, however, with whom I eventually became good friends, he had, completely coincidentally, been publishing a 'zine named *Quimby* in Boston for five years while I was drawing my *Quimby the Mouse* strips in Texas. Steven eventually asked me to redesign the building's signage, so I exploited the parallels and granted unlimited, in-perpetuity use of my two-headed mouse character to the store." —Chris Ware, cartoonist/writer/artist, *Building Stories*

LIBRAIRIE AVANT-GARDE

NANJING, CHINA
1999 TO PRESENT

To find Librairie Avant-Garde, book lovers must drive on a mysterious road that leads, as if in a James Bond movie, down a hill and into an enormous underground bunker—the site of a former bomb shelter. The space later became a parking garage before it became the world's largest "hidden" bookshop (at 43,000 square feet). Lines form outside to enter the shop every day. Once inside you continue to follow a double-yellow-striped road to the main room of Librairie Avant-Garde, where you will find three hundred chairs to read in, a coffee shop, an event space, a replica of Rodin's *The Thinker*, and literally miles of books.

The tunnel entrance is lined
with books and one goes under a huge black Christian cross.

The owner converted to Christianity after he
opened his first bookstore,
and he kept hearing the hymns from St. Paul's
Cathedral, which was across the street.
The owner, Qian Xiaocha, has said, "Reading is our religion,
and this place is the heaven for book lovers."

POSMAN BOOKS

NEW YORK CITY
1995 TO PRESENT

Posman Books sell books at three locations in New York City and is family-owned. This location, inside Grand Central Station, closed in 2014 much to the sadness of many a busy commuter. A new location opened on Wall Street not long after. It was voted Best Bookstore in 2012 by *New York* magazine.

"I was looking out the front window and saw a crowd of people screaming and shouting as they ran up the ramp going to Forty-second and Vanderbilt—I figured that something bad must be happening in the station. Seconds later, just like in a Marx Brothers routine, they all came running back down, still shouting. We quickly asked the customers to leave and then locked the doors, evacuating through a rear entrance. When we reached the street, the sky was red and thick with dust—I thought a plane had hit a skyscraper or that a building across from Grand Central was on fire. We finally learned from watching a TV through a bar's window that a ConEdison steam pipe had exploded on Park. White dust drifted down onto our hair and clothes; we found out later that it was asbestos. A couple of days later, some customers who had left in a panic came back and paid for the books they had accidentally taken with them." —Ron Kolm, poet, former manager at Posman Books Grand Central

BOOK CULTURE

NEW YORK CITY
1997 TO PRESENT

———

Book Culture has three stores on the Upper West Side of Manhattan. Two of the stores occupy spaces where neighborhood favorites Endicott Booksellers and Morningside Books once operated. It was voted *TimeOut's* Best Store of 2014 Upper West Side.

"The philosopher Marshall Berman was incredibly comfortable with himself and would completely give in to whatever he was reading. He would come in, start to browse, and then you would notice he was deeply reading for an hour or more. As time went by on these afternoons, he would go lower and lower, from a standing position to a leaning slant and then sit right down. From the seated position he would lie down on his side on the concrete floor in the aisle with a philosophy book in one hand and a great, bearded shaggy head propped in the other without a care in the world." —Chris Doeblin, owner

BODHI TREE BOOKSTORE

HOLLYWOOD, CALIFORNIA
1970–2011

Bodhi Tree Bookstore in Hollywood was one of the first, and certainly one of the largest and most extensive, spiritual-themed bookstores in the United States. It closed on New Year's Eve 2011.

The store's genesis began in the late 1960s when three Douglas Aircraft employees became interested in transcendental meditation and Buddhism. Dan Morris and remaining owners Phil Thompson and Stan Madson were working on weapons of mass destruction before starting the store in their thirties. The trio opened Bodhi Tree as a spiritual center and bookstore in 1970.

The Bodhi Tree Bookstore was a founding sponsor of the *Los Angeles Times* Book Fair. In the early 1980s, actress Shirley MacLaine dropped by, changed her life, the life of the bookstore, and a significant portion of the spiritual thinking in America. Her bookstore visits became a TV series and a bestselling book, *Out on a Limb*.

"I frequented the Bodhi Tree occasionally when in L.A. In 1986 or so I took Michael Jackson to the Bodhi Tree Bookstore in West Hollywood to browse. He was in disguise dressed as an Arab woman with headscarf and veil. Some people stared as we looked like a strange couple. We bought several books of Carlos Castaneda and a copy of Yogananda's *Autobiography of a Yogi*. I have a picture of us in a limousine on our way back to Solvang [California], tired and sleepy after an evening of innocent fun."
—Deepak Chopra

SHAKESPEARE AND COMPANY

PARIS, FRANCE
1919–1941
REOPENED 1951 TO PRESENT

True bibliophiles consider Shakespeare and Company to be the world's greatest bookstore. The original store was operated by American Sylvia Beach at 12 rue de l'Odéon. Beach was the first publisher of James Joyce's modern masterwork *Ulysses*.

In 1951, another American, George Whitman, opened a bookshop called Le Mistral at 37 rue de la Bûcherie. Whitman changed his store's name to Shakespeare and Company in 1964, both to honor Beach's original shop and to commemorate the four-hundredth anniversary of William Shakespeare's birth. The shop became a meeting place, clubhouse, and post office for writers such as Ezra Pound, James Joyce, T. S. Eliot, and many others. Whitman's daughter, Sylvia, now runs the landmark. The shop estimates that about 30,000 aspiring writers have slept at Shakespeare and Company over the decades.

"When I was 17, I graduated school early and took off to Paris, where I dreamed of somehow getting into the Shakespeare and Company world. I was horrifically shy though. Instead of speaking to people I'd sit beneath the cherry tree in front of the store, drawing. One day, George shambled up to me in his perfectly rumpled, dapper suit and said, 'There is no miracle greater than to be a young girl in Paris in the spring.' I ended up living there months on and off, in that anarchist dictatorship that changed my life."

—Molly Crabapple, *Drawing Blood*

Noel Riley Fitch famously wrote a book of the shop's storied past. One story from *Sylvia Beach and the Lost Generation* tells of Ernest Hemingway being too nervous to do a book event alone—he got his writer friend to speak with him. That wasn't enough, and he started off stammering and the Who's Who audience asked that he speak up. With the help of whiskey and beer under the table, he began reading with confidence and grace with "a strong American accent."

The book also explains the store's closing in December 1941, when one day a gray military car pulled up to Shakespeare and Company. A German officer requested in perfect English to buy the *Finnegans Wake* displayed in the window. "It's not for sale," Sylvia Beach said of her last personal copy. The officer returned at the end of the month, and when he was again denied, he threatened that all the books would be confiscated and stormed off. As soon as the officer drove off, Beach, with the help of writers Maurice Saillet and Adrienne Monnier (Beach's life partner) and a concierge, moved tables, chairs, signs, and 5,000 books up four flights of stairs into hiding. Shakespeare and Company was gone in two hours.

Patrons have included Allen Ginsberg, Henry Miller, Richard Wright, Langston Hughes, Lawrence Durrell, Anaïs Nin, James Jones, William Styron, Ray Bradbury, Julio Cortázar, James Baldwin, Gregory Corso, Martin Amis, Carol Ann Duffy, Paul Auster, Philip Pullman, Lydia Davis, Charles Simi, A.M. Homes, Darin Strauss, and Frank Sinatra.

George Whitman, who hated to pay for haircuts, used to trim his hair by burning it by candles. He once threw a party and invited the equally shy Samuel Beckett; the two men spent the night just staring at each other.

"I grew up here, amongst the dust and the broken spines of old classics, and so Shakespeare and Company will always have a thousand fond memories for me. And the wonderful thing about the bookshop is that it keeps giving me memories, day after day. It could be anything; two of our resident tumbleweeds drawing a crowd in the cold outside the shop singing Dylan songs with their buck-toothed old guitars or the time author Nathan Englander got married here."
—Sylvia Whitman, owner

Myrsine and Hélène Moschos, Sylvia Beach,

and Ernest Hemingway

BRATTLE BOOK SHOP

BOSTON, MASSACHUSETTS
1825 TO PRESENT

Owned by Ken Gloss of *Antiques Roadshow*, Brattle Book Shop has a history that dates back to 1825, and has been in the hands of the Gloss family since 1949. It is so important in the book-buying world that the *customers* will call in sick if they can't make it to the Boston shop.

"There's a woman who regularly buys bibles from us to eat so that she can have the word of God in her."

"Once a customer came in asking for Richard Yates. When he left, my employee of one week informed me, 'That was J. D. Salinger—I dated his daughter.'"

"One vivid memory I have is an ecstatic student shouting when he found on one of the outside racks a book on coconuts and constipation."

"In 1969 my father had to move and empty the store. As a promotion we had a horse-drawn carriage announcing 'Go West' to lead people to the store. Lines went around the block and we rang bells to give people five minutes to grab what they could and then give others a chance in the store. We gave away 250,000 books." —Ken Gloss

MARTINUS

MARTIN, SLOVAKIA
1990 TO PRESENT

The Martinus bookstore chain was founded in Martin, Slovakia, in 1990 by two brothers shortly after the Velvet Revolution (a nonviolent upheaval of power in what was then Czechoslovakia). The original tiny bookshop has since grown into the largest bookstore in Slovakia, the largest Slovak online bookstore, and second largest chain of brick and mortar bookstores (six in total).

Their stores are famous for their delightful interiors. One features playful book references throughout, such as tributes to Isaac Asimov's "three laws of robotics," as well as nods to *The Hitchhiker's Guide to the Galaxy*, *The Lord of the Rings*, and *Harry Potter*.

"We have this concept of 'WOW moments'
that we aim to provide our customers.
New ones are happening every day,"
says manager Michal Brat. An example was in 2015 when
the store held a contest of who could find the most
hidden book references within the store's huge
elaborate mural (there were 64).

MOE'S BOOKS

BERKELEY, CALIFORNIA
1959 TO PRESENT

———————

Moe's Books is a cultural institution and played an integral part
in Berkeley's Beatnik free-speech anti-Vietnam war past.

"Part of my job as a clerk at Moe's, in the early '90s, was to scour the massive wall of fiction and confront the books that weren't selling. Out of all the staff I claimed this task because it interested me the most and because it suited my vanity to be able to claim that 'I run the lit section.' Codes, written in pencil, and discreetly tucked into the corner opposite the asking price, revealed when a given title had hit the shelf. After six or eight months, you reduced the price. Once it had been knocked down a couple of times, two options remained: chuck the book into the pile of discards under the staircase, or take it home and read it."

—Jonathan Lethem

GROLIER POETRY BOOK SHOP

CAMBRIDGE, MASSACHUSETTS
1927 TO PRESENT

The Grolier Poetry Book Shop is the oldest continuously existing poetry bookstore in the United States. It is owned by the Nigerian poet Professor Ifeanyi Menkiti, who attended school around the corner at Harvard and has taught at Wellesley College for over forty years. His nonprofit Grolier Poetry Foundation publishes and supports poets of note.

I asked Menkiti, sitting in the middle of his small, elegant shop, what first attracted him to poetry. "Back in college, Berkeley," he answered. "It was Ezra Pound's *The Cantos.* The rhythm when he talks about the War of Roses. Canto Eighty: Boom boom, boom boom. It brought me back to memories of royal African drums. Music resides inside the human tribes of the world, and the tears that the nations cry, their joys, it's as if they're not able to cry or have their joy unless they encode it in song. Growing up in Nigeria, there was a lot of song in the air. I believe strongly that poetry can still help heal the world."

THREE LIVES & COMPANY

NEW YORK CITY

1968 TO PRESENT

Named after Gertrude Stein's first published book, Three Lives & Company is perched on a Greenwich Village street corner.

At six hundred square feet, it's the size of a luxurious Park Avenue closet.
"Any time a book is bought, the entire shelf must be rearranged
since no books of the same color spine may be adjacent lest
they appear erroneously as a set." —Toby Cox, owner

Pulitzer Prize winner Michael Cunningham once said he wanted to be buried
under the store, but the owners at the time told him they weren't zoned for that.

BOOKHAMPTON

LONG ISLAND, NEW YORK
1971 TO PRESENT

———

Bookhampton is a family-owned bookshop located in both East Hampton and Southampton, New York. At its height, Bookhampton also had stores in Amagansett, Bridgehampton, and Mattituck. This store, along with the famed Canio's Books, served a neighborhood blessed with literary giants including Kurt Vonnegut, E. L. Doctorow, Robert Caro, Jason Epstein, George Plimpton, Truman Capote, and John Steinbeck.

The Clintons' favorite bookstore has had many ups and downs, frequently up for sale and changing hands. But a highlight was Hillary's book signing in 2014 when a thousand plus lined up through East Hampton to meet the possible future president. Nothing dampened the mood of giddy fans waiting all day, not even getting frisked by the Secret Service.

BOOK CELLAR

CHICAGO, ILLINOIS
2004 TO PRESENT

The Book Cellar has become a staple in Chicago's literary scene. It was named for the owner's love of books and wine.

Book Cellar

"The Book Cellar marries two very scholastic pastimes, reading and getting sauced on wine." —Heather Crothall, *Harbinger*

"Four comfy chairs beckon by the Book Cellar's display window. A recent bout of depression sidelined me from many writerly pursuits. But in those plush chairs, I convalesced back to intellectual health. I watched passersby in the Lincoln Square twilight. I read *Atlantic* editor Scott Stossel's *My Age of Anxiety* and felt hope. I scribbled random bitches about health that birthed poems of...rebirth. Relentless dread needs a cure: a place to read (and write) new chapters." —Lou Carlozo, professor of journalism at National Louis University

WORD ON THE WATER

LONDON, ENGLAND
2011 TO PRESENT

Word on the Water is London's only floating secondhand bookshop. In 2015 it was finally granted a mooring at King's Cross, Granary Square. The one-hundred-year-old Dutch book barge hosts poetry slams, book readings, and live music events on the roof stage on top of the boat. Steven Fry and Russell Brand are among the well known who have been on board.

"Back in 2002, I was evicted from my squat in Hackney, which was auctioned and the buyer had to pay us to leave. I used my share on a boat. It was an old 1950s Norfolk Broads cruiser, half-sunk, which took a lot of looking after and then literally fell apart one night. So I bought an ex-police boat (by borrowing some money off my mum) that I kept for seven years, during which time I acquired this one.

I planned the Word on the Water business with my friend Paddy: seeing this boat for sale, but not able to afford it, we asked the seller if we could rent it and then he turned around and said he'd sell us the boat for a share in the business. So we own a third each. It's shockingly expensive to live on a boat in London but still a fraction of what it costs to live in a house." —Captain Jon Privett, owner

JOHN K. KING USED & RARE BOOKS

DETROIT, MICHIGAN
1965 TO PRESENT

Located in Detroit, Michigan, in a former glove factory left over from the 1940s, John K. King Used & Rare Books was established in 1965. It has four floors of maze-like aisles of books, and much of the original glove signage has been preserved in this, one of the largest bookshops in the United States. It is frequently mentioned on "Best of" lists as one of the most beautiful bookstores in the world.

The shop owns a first edition of the *Book of Mormon*, priced at $100,000, and a copy of the writings of St. Thomas Aquinas printed in Venice in 1482.

Also available for sale: a pair of letters from Elsa Einstein, Albert's wife, to one of Einstein's mistresses for $5,000.

"The last time the late great William Safire came to our bookstore, he got so preoccupied with the books that he almost missed a radio interview; we had to rush him uptown, running through red lights, just to get him to the gig before it was too late. Luckily we were driving an old police car."
—John King, owner

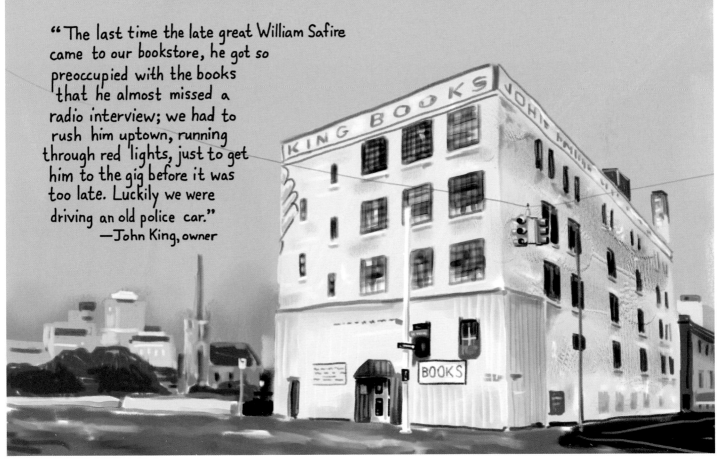

GIGGLES

CHENNAI, INDIA
1974 TO PRESENT

Its store sign proudly announces GIGGLES: BIGGEST LITTLE BOOK SHOP, and it is listed by Lonely Planet as a "must see" in Chennai, India. The cramped one-hundred-square-foot bookstore is run by Nalini Chettur, well known in Chennai English literary circles. In 2003, Chettur was given the Best Bookseller Award by the Booksellers and Publishers Association of South India.

Giggles

BIGGEST LITTLE BOOK SHOP

VOLTAS

"Perhaps my favorite all-time shop. Originally housed in the elegant lobby of the four-starred Taj hotel, there must have been some kind of major brouhaha and the Taj kicked Nalini out, but not entirely—I suspect she had some fans who could not be ignored. Her shop is now on 'the grounds' of the Taj in the parking lot. You can't actually enter the shop easily; there are more books than there is space—stacks upon stacks, so each day she chooses the twenty or so books to feature. These books are displayed on the sidewalk in front of the shop, the lovely owner holds court from her lawn chair, and a charming literary salon ensues until the mosquitos and it's time to run for shelter." —Susan Donnelly, Harvard University Press

PAGEANT BOOK & PRINT SHOP

NEW YORK CITY
1946–1999

———

The Pageant Book & Print Shop on Twelfth Street in Manhattan was in business from 1946 to 1999 until it became an online store. It has since returned as a small print shop on Fourth Street.

When Sharon Mesmer first moved to New York City, she went straight here, hoping to find a book that would serve as a gateway to her new life as an acclaimed New York poet. "The way it looked in 'Hannah and Her Sisters,' it had to be the first bookstore I set foot in. In the nether-most corner, a book fell on my head: 'Ways to Self-Realization,' by Mouni Sadhu, the spiritual nom de plume, I later discovered, of a Polish author named—wait for it—Mieczyslaw Demetriusz Sudowski. I opened it to a random page, and the first words (in caps) were 'WE ARE NOT THE MIND.' I thought, well, it has nothing to do with literature, but I'll bet anything I'm going to need it later. When I finally opened it again, twenty-three years later, during a nervous break-down, I was right." — Sharon Mesmer

WORD BOOKSTORE

BROOKLYN, NEW YORK
2007 TO PRESENT

WORD Bookstore of Greenpoint in Brooklyn expanded to a second
location in Jersey City, New Jersey, in 2013.

Missed Connection posted on Craigslist, "We spotted each other at WORD. I don't think you followed me but we ended up in the park afterward. You sat next to me on a bench as the sun was beginning to set. You were reading Willa Cather and I was reading Edward St. Aubyn. Our knees touched once and later quietly stayed that way.

It was the most romantic thing I'd ever felt. I knew we were both too shy to ever say anything to one another and I regret it badly now. I'd love a million more days in the park like that one with you. I came back an hour later but you were gone. Find me. Please." WORD then played matchmaker and tweeted, "VERY IMPORTANT, if you shopped at the Brooklyn store yesterday…"

LIVING BATCH BOOKSTORE

ALBUQUERQUE, NEW MEXICO
1970–1996

A great supporter of authors, poets, and small-press enthusiasts, Phil Mayne opened the Yale Street Grasshopper in Albuquerque, New Mexico, in 1967 and sold Beat and American contemporary poetry and underground papers. In 1970, the Grasshopper changed ownership and became Living Batch Bookstore. ("How the Batch got its name?" Pancho Elliston, an early owner says: "It's from Ed Dorn's poem *Gunslinger*. Gunslinger injected into a dead person five gallons of acid. He awoke and became 'a living batch.'")

After Elliston, the essayist Gus Blaisdell took ownership from 1976 until its closure on Christmas Eve 1996. In 1978, Batch got a phone and in 1988, a cash register. "There was no gay, no women, no politics, no black, no small-press poetry, no serious literature in the state," Blaisdell said about the store's early years. Authors who frequented the Batch ranged from Henry Rollins to Allen Ginsberg to Mary Higgins Clark.

"I spent my life as a teenager here because the guy who owned it was a mentor to me, a guy named Gus, Gus Blaisdell. There was one time I walked in and there was a poster on the wall there for a conference at the Naropa Institute. At that time the idea around Naropa was there was some sort of extension of the Beatnik model. It was Allen Ginsberg, William S. Burroughs, among a list of people who were going to be up there, and I was, early on in college, very much into hero worshipping of those guys, and I was like, 'Oh, man, I gotta get up there and make that road trip to see them,' but Gus was standing there behind the counter, he was sort of from that generation, maybe a little younger, and said, 'Why are you going up to watch those geriatrics for? Why don't you do *your* thing?' That was a moment for me. I don't know what I wanted from these people but for him to say that was mind-blowing for me somehow." —Marc Maron

ADOBE BOOKS

SAN FRANCISCO, CALIFORNIA
1989 TO PRESENT

Located in San Francisco's Mission District, Adobe Books describes itself on its website as "not a bookshop. It is not an art gallery. It is not a living room. It is not a retail store. It is not a community center. It is not a place to meet new friends. It does not have comfy chairs. It does not have a community table. It does not have art and music events. It is not possibly one of the world's best bookstores. It is not a co-operative run business. —*Adobe Books & Arts Cooperative, defying definitions since 1989.*"

In 2013, the store's rent was set to practically double in the fast-gentrifying neighborhood. The artist community that had grown up around Adobe over the decades promptly rallied, and once starving, now influential artists like Rebecca Solnit and Chris Johanson took over the store as a collective.

"The most amazing show they ever had was in 2004 when artist Chris Cobb rearranged the entire store in order of color—rainbow hues, and then a big black-and-white section," said artist Scott Snibbe.

Cobb reorganized 20,000 books with the help of roughly 15 volunteers, overnight, beginning at 10 p.m. Friday and finishing at 8 a.m. Saturday, so as not to disrupt normal business. And 24,000 tags with shelf and row numbers were printed so that the books could be returned to their original places.

MOBY DICKENS BOOKSHOP

TAOS, NEW MEXICO
1984-2015

Moby Dickens was a premier independent bookshop in Taos, New Mexico, specializing in rare and out-of-print books about the Southwest and very active in the local writing community.

"A town without a bookstore
is a town without a soul." —Lucy Dillon, *Lost Dogs and Lonely Hearts*,
as quoted on Moby Dickens's website

"My apologies for the delay.
We have been fighting tooth and nail to keep the shop running, so my focus has been skewed to say the
least. Unfortunately, we will be forced to close the shop within the next fifteen to thirty days. Economic
conditions in our town continue to deteriorate, and the overwhelming power of online shopping on the book business
is the greatest piece of our inability to continue operating. People are happy when they come in,
but want you to have the resources and pricing of online or they won't buy." —Jay Moore, owner

HARVARD BOOK STORE

CAMBRIDGE, MASSACHUSETTS
1932 TO PRESENT

Founded in 1932, Harvard Book Store is a Boston-area institution and destination for book buyers across the country.

In 2009, it unveiled Paige M. Gutenborg, its on-site printing machine that can print books in under four minutes. The event was hosted by E. L. Doctorow, who stated the machine "may indeed be an answer to all the people who foresee the end of the physical book as words becoming ones and zeros and appearing on screens. I hope the little man inside that machine really knows what he's doing." As its first book, Gutenborg printed a facsimile of the first edition of *The Whole Booke of Psalmes Faithfully Translated into English Metre*, commonly known as the Bay Psalm Book, the first book ever printed in the American colonies, in Cambridge, 1640.

"I worked in the used department...one time a woman came in to sell a bunch of old books and a picture fell out of one of them: it was a picture of her, naked, in the midst of a strip poker game. She slammed her hand down on the counter and covered it, then took it and ripped it up and threw it in the trash can—our trash can, so of course once she left we plucked it out and taped it back together."

—Davy Rothbart, *Found: The Best Lost, Tossed, and Forgotten Items from Around the World*

BÓKIN

REYKJAVÍK, ICELAND
1964 TO PRESENT

Meaning "the book," Bókin was founded in Reykjavík, Iceland, in 1964. The shop specializes in books for Icelandic and international collectors and museums. It has been called a "1950s version of New York's Strand bookstore."

Bókin was Bobby Fischer's favorite bookstore after his 1972 victory in Iceland over Boris Spassky. The polarizing former World Chess Champion moved to Iceland in March of 2005 where he became a hermit and paranoid in the last years of his life, even having his mail sometimes delivered to the store instead of his Reykjavik apartment. He would spend hours in the back of the store, where he sometimes fell asleep.

BOOKS OF WONDER

NEW YORK CITY
1980 TO PRESENT

Books of Wonder's claim to fame is that it was the model for the bookstore in the 1997 film *You've Got Mail*. Nora and Delia Ephron, who wrote the film, were both longtime customers and friends of the store—and Meg Ryan spent a day working at the shop to prepare for her role in the film. In 1985, Books of Wonder established a joint imprint with William Morrow and Company, publishing its own children's books. Its standing-room-only events have included celebrated authors like J. K. Rowling, Madeleine L'Engle, Maurice Sendak, and Eric Carle.

"My very first book signing was like a dream. Held at the famous Books of Wonder in Manhattan, I shared a table with the great Lane Smith. The first customer was an adorable little girl who, clutching her book very tightly, approached me with an angelic smile. As she gazed up at me with a look of adoration and pure love, her father bent down and said, 'No, dear. Lane Smith is the other guy.' The smile immediately devolved into a quick, hideous grimace as she zipped over to the other end of the table. I can still recall her face as if she was the only person to approach me that day, because she was." —Mo Willems

POWELL'S BOOKS

PORTLAND, OREGON
1971 TO PRESENT

Powell's Books has five locations in Portland, Oregon. The store boasts over a million volumes with approximately 80,000 shoppers every day in its 68,000-square-foot store and more via its robust online shop.

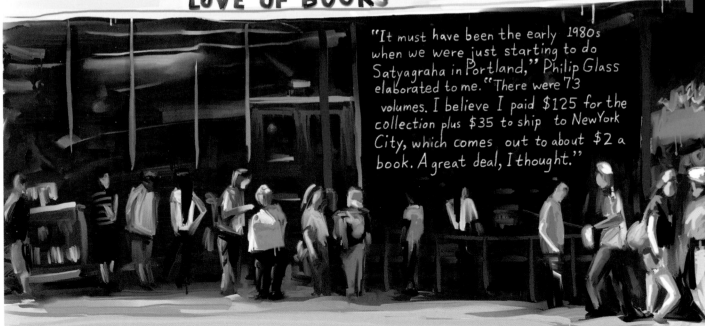

"Philip Glass bought a Gandhi set here and is still working his way through them."
—Kim Sutton, Powell's

POWELL'S BOOKS
USED & NEW BOOKS
FOR THE
LOVE OF BOOKS

"It must have been the early 1980s when we were just starting to do Satyagraha in Portland," Philip Glass elaborated to me. "There were 73 volumes. I believe I paid $125 for the collection plus $35 to ship to New York City, which comes out to about $2 a book. A great deal, I thought."

MORAVIAN BOOK SHOP

BETHLEHEM, PENNSYLVANIA
1745 TO PRESENT

The Moravian Book Shop was established by Bethlehem Inn keeper Samuel Powell at the insistence of the bishop of the Moravian Church in Bethlehem, who desired Powell to import and distribute books. It is the oldest continuously operating book shop in the world. Other establishments have made this claim, such as the Bertrand bookshop (established 1732), but the Great Lisbon Earthquake of 1755 precipitated its closing for eight years until it reopened in 1773. Korn & Berg of Nuremberg, Germany, dates back to 1531, tenuously, as it changed locations and names and was leveled by World War II bombings. The Moravian Book Shop is also America's oldest store.

Some 270 years later, the 14,000-square-foot shop expanded to a second shop in Allentown, Pennsylvania. The two bookshops are still associated with the church.

Charles Dickens's great-great-grandson, actor Gerald Charles Dickens, played twenty-six characters during a presentation held by the shop of the elder Dickens's 1843 classic *A Christmas Carol.*

"I was at the Moravian bookstore today [for a book signing] and the book buyer, Janelle Locket, explained every book you buy in a local book store affects the economy in seven different ways. Independent bookstores are a dying breed in this country, but I think we can bring them back, like vinyl recordings and having someone pump gas for you and having shoes that are made by people and stuff like that." —Greg Proops, comedian, *The Smartest Man in the World*

GOTHAM BOOK MART

NEW YORK CITY
1920–2007

———

Gotham Book Mart was a meeting place for the literati and many twentieth-century cultural icons. Frances Steloff was one of the world's most distinguished independent booksellers. In 2008, the University of Pennsylvania received over 200,000 items from its inventory as an anonymous gift.

Great names in literature were not just on the shelves but were also customers: Saul Bellow, Truman Capote, E. E. Cummings, James Joyce, Norman Mailer, Eugene O'Neill, Anaïs Nin, George Plimpton, Philip Roth, J. D. Salinger, the list goes on. Even the store's clerks were noteworthy and included Allen Ginsberg, LeRoi Jones, Abigail Folger, Patti Smith, and once, for less than a day, Tennessee Williams.

"One time I saw an old fedora lying on the top shelf of a closet where I was putting away some first editions. I put it on my head and it fit perfectly. 'Andy [Brown, rare book dealer of the Gotham Book Mart at the time],' I said, 'whose hat is this? Can I have this?' He looked up from his work and said, 'You take that hat off right away; it was E. E. Cummings's.'"—Matthew Tannenbaum, *My Years at The Gotham Book Mart with Frances Steloff, Proprietor*

16   GOTHAM BOOK M

"Once when driving in the snow on my way to the *New Yorker*, I picked up two pretty hitchhikers with heavy brogues—fashion graduates from Dublin—who wanted to see New York City. I dropped them off at Gotham and caught up with them later. We sat on the floor in the back of the store and ate sandwiches, read Irish poetry, and finished a six-pack of Harp Lager together. It was so tasty there. The James Joyce Society was meeting in the back in the Anna La Bella something Room...Edward Gorey sometimes behind the register... his art was hanging in their gallery...you have to understand, back then going to a bookstore was a treat, equal to going to a concert."

—Arnie Levin, *New Yorker* cartoonist

ART & GALLERY   16

WEAPON OF MASS INSTRUCTION

ARGENTINA
2003 TO PRESENT

Artist Raul Lemesoff converted a 1979 Ford Falcon with a turret into a mobile bookstore tank carrying over nine hundred selections. His first peace tank, Arma de Instruccion Masiva (Weapon of Mass Instruction), toured the United States.

In 2004 he built a second one, designed to transport more than 2,500 books, which travels in Buenos Aires, Argentina, handing out books for free to people on the street. The tank's supply comes from public book donations.

In 2010 he was commissioned to build a third Weapon of Mass Instruction in The Hague, Netherlands.

"Culture within sculpture."
—Raul Lemesoff, artist

ELLIOTT BAY BOOK COMPANY

SEATTLE, WASHINGTON
1973 TO PRESENT

––––––––––

The Elliott Bay Book Company is an independent, family-owned bookstore credited for getting big-house publishers to send writers as far as the West and Northwest.

"President Bill Clinton arrived in a limo with a pack of secret service men. He spent forty-five minutes shopping, reading in every section and taking time to say hello to all the customers. I remember him greeting a couple from France.
   He said his favorite thing to do was spending Sundays reading on the Truman porch." —Tracy Taylor, General Manager

BOOKS & BOOKS

SOUTH FLORIDA
1982 TO PRESENT

———————

Books & Books is a trio of independent book stores in Coral Gables, Miami Beach, and Bal Harbour, with additional affiliate stores in southern Florida hosting up to sixty author events a month.

"One night when I was just about to close, my bookseller, George Henry Keen, tapped me on the back of my shoulder and said these seven magic words, 'Paul McCartney needs your help in fiction.' I showed him (his pregnant wife, and two bodyguards) around the store, but he was most interested in anything Dickens. He fondly remembered the Penguin editions he read at university and regaled me with stories of a particular literature professor who had a great influence on him." —Mitchell Kaplan, owner

TRAVELER RESTAURANT—FOOD AND BOOKS

UNION, CONNECTICUT

1985 TO PRESENT

Straddling the Connecticut and Massachusetts border off of highway I-84, the Traveler Restaurant has given away over two million books to diners. After your meal you pick any three books from the restaurant/bookstore for free.

"Bill Murray was here recently dancing to the music playing. We've had Robert Ludlum, Robin Moore, and Bruce Springsteen visit...now when a limousine pulls up we wonder, What big celebrity could this be now? Most of the time it's just a limo driver needing a break." —Art Murdock, owner

ZWEITAUSENDEINS

FRANKFURT, GERMANY
1969 TO PRESENT

Opened in 1969, Zweitausendeins was once a major player in publishing in Germany, selling new and out-of-print books as well as music. But it was important politically as well, being often the only outlet for certain counterculture content in this region.

There were many physical stores throughout Germany, but since 1974, they are mostly mail-order bookstores using a cheap monthly shopping catalog, called the "Merheft."

"Every Merheft would contain a personal short note on the back page by Frau Susemihl, a lady working for Zweitausendeins. They showed the very same photo of her for 30 years, so everyone wondered whether she is fake or real. Actually, she indeed was a real person but died in 1997 at age 90 shortly after retiring. Zweitausendeins was one of the legends of my teenage days offering books for incredibly low prices, allowing teenagers to buy a library he/she could never have afforded. However, it was not only the prices that made Zweitausendeins so attractive—they precisely hit the needs of the revolutionary, protesting, hippie, pop, philosophical, sex revolution, feminist, upcoming green teenager lifestyle as no other store."

—Professor Michael Reichling, University of Osnabrück

MYOPIC BOOKS

CHICAGO, ILLINOIS
1990 TO PRESENT

One of Chicago's largest used bookstores, Myopic Books has three floors of books with over 70,000 editions.

"Myopic has a great used book selection and the most rules you will find in any bookstore. Many people are afraid to go in. They are the *Seinfeld* Soup Nazi of bookstores."—anonymous loyal customer

I couldn't get them to respond to my emails and phone calls so I went to this Chicago store in person, twice (for the record, I live in New York City). I still couldn't get anyone to speak to me. I can't help it, this only made me think of them as even more special, like that girl in high school who won't speak to you.

ST. MARK'S BOOKSHOP

EAST VILLAGE, NEW YORK CITY
1977–2016

———

St. Mark's Bookshop was established in New York City's East Village in 1977 and moved four times within the neighborhood, finally closing in 2016.

"Madonna came in with Sean Penn, who used to buy Bukowski there. I don't think I would have noticed them except that I was thinking, That woman's hair is an unusual color of blond. Then she turned around and it was Madonna. Our guy at the register had been a club doorman, so he knew her. He mentioned to Madonna that there was a picture of her in a photography book on the display table, but he couldn't find the picture. She said, 'I hate it when a guy gets me all interested and then doesn't come through,' while Sean Penn glared daggers."

—Terry McCoy, owner

GARDEN DISTRICT BOOK SHOP

NEW ORLEANS, LOUISIANA

1980 TO PRESENT

Garden District Book Shop resides inside the historic property called the Rink in the beautiful New Orleans Garden District.

Anne Rice once arrived at a book signing at the shop by means of a jazz funeral procession in an antique hearse pulled by mules. She emerged in the bookstore from inside the closed coffin.

TELL A STORY

PORTUGAL
2013 TO PRESENT

———

This vintage van specializes in showcasing English translations of local Portuguese authors that in some cases it publishes itself and for which it created a downloadable font based on the handwriting of Portuguese writers.

"Portugal was born with the gift of writing...
[we're] a bookshop that does not know how to remain
in the same place." —Domingos Cruz, Tell a Story owner

THE ANTIQUARIUM BOOKSTORE

BROWNVILLE, NEBRASKA
1969 TO PRESENT

The Antiquarium Bookstore is one of the few "Book Towns" in the United States, rural towns with a large number of used book or antiquarian bookstores where bibliophiles gather and literary festivals take place. Others include Archer City, Texas; Stillwater, Minnesota; and Hobart, New York.

"What I loved was the hospitality there. The bookstore is/was run by a sort of legendary fellow in my mind and life...a little otherworldly, ethereal, anachronistically pursuing gentility...changed my impression of what people were like in the middle of the country. So kind and generous and thinky. Twice I slept at the bookstore, snuggling in the aisles with my traveling companions, my then boyfriends. I remember the bookshelves looming above us forever and ever, like skyscrapers. I remember feeling like the books were maps to other people and other times and other lives. I've slept in other bookstores—I stayed at Shakespeare and Company in Paris, and I napped at Pistil Books in Seattle. But only at Antiquarium did I feel a sense of what the library at Alexandria might have been: an accumulation of evidence and suggestions."

—Amy Halloran, *The New Bread Basket*

PARNASSUS BOOKS

NASHVILLE, TENNESSEE
2011 TO PRESENT

Parnassus Books is an independent bookstore in Nashville, Tennessee, co-owned by Karen Hayes and bestselling author Ann Patchett.

Parnassus has a piano and publishes a literary magazine, and in 2016 they launched a bookmobile, having bought a van from a library in Georgia on eBay. The bookshop has partnered with schools, universities, businesses, and nonprofit organizations for fundraisers, and its literary series attracts major authors—like Doris Kearns Goodwin, Donna Tartt, and Caroline Kennedy—to the city. It also cosponsors Nashville Reads, an annual event that gets the whole city to read the same book.

"I have no interest in retail; I have no interest in opening a bookstore. But I also have no interest in living in a city without a bookstore."

—Ann Patchett, who also once famously made a plea for the value of indies on *The Colbert Report*

FORBIDDEN PLANET

NEW YORK CITY
1978 TO PRESENT

———————

One of the world's largest sellers of sci-fi and comics, Forbidden Planet has been in business since 1978 and now has thirty stores worldwide. It started in London where there are now nine locations and the flagship megastore, which is a city landmark. The New York City location is the city's only branch, making it an important source of sci-fi literature and a tourist attraction.

"Clive Barker was promoting his movie 'Hellraiser' when a punk kid off the street cut open his own arm with a knife and asked Barker for an autograph in his blood. Clive obliged by dipping his pen in the blood dripping from the kid's arm. Years later, Barker returned to the store for an event and was asked whether he remembered the bizarre kid. 'Yes, he's a square living in California—we're friends now.'"
—Jeff Ayers, manager

LIVRARIA LELLO

PORTO, PORTUGAL
1869 TO PRESENT

———

The original establishment began nearby and moved a couple of times before opening at its current building in 1906. Designed by Xavier Esteves, Livraria Lello is still one of the most beautiful bookstores in the world. The facade is an excellent example of neo-Gothic design, and its interior features Art Nouveau carved wood panels, arches, and columns, stained glass ceilings, glass bookshelves, and a curvaceous, twisting, store-long staircase.

The staircase is said to have inspired the famous moving staircase in *Harry Potter*—J. K. Rowling wrote from 1991 to 1993 while an English teacher in Porto. Pillars are ornamented with bronze bas-relief figures from Portuguese literature. Above the windows are paintings of figures by José Bielman.

WORDSWORTH BOOKS

CAMBRIDGE, MASSACHUSETTS
1976–2005

———

Cambridge's WordsWorth Books was one of the innovative forces in the modernization of the bookselling landscape. It created a computer-driven inventory system for bookstores that is still used today.

Store owner Hillel Stavis shared with me two challenges he recalls: "Ed was bipolar and, sadly, did smell like something long dead. He lived under our staircase for 20 years and some cold nights, inside the store. Employees brought him food and shoes. I'll tell you, it wasn't always good for business, but that's what we did.

I also remember when Salman Rushdie was to speak at WordsWorth but the fatwa against him was called, forcing him into hiding. Instead we organized a panel to discuss the fatwa and publishers' and booksellers' responsibility to keep his books on the shelves vs. threats of retaliation for selling his work. Rushdie did come back to read after he came out of hiding."

SPRING STREET BOOKS

NEW YORK CITY
1979–1998

Spring Street Books of New York City was originally called New Morning until 1984. Spring Street was owned by Tom Forcade—journalist, activist, and founder of *High Times* magazine.

One-time manager, full-time poet Ron Kolm says that regulars included Spalding Gray, Art Spiegelman, David Byrne, Susan Sontag ("very nice"), Joe Jackson ("very tall; no one ever recognized him"), Madonna, Joan Jett, Larry Kramer, Laurie Anderson, Brian Eno, Billy Idol, Thurston Moore, and Tuli Kupferberg. "Kathy Acker would use our only phone and tie it up for hours. We couldn't order books or anything until we got her to leave. We did like her a lot, though... I was behind the register reading an issue of *Punk Magazine* with David Johansen in the store. He got such a kick out of that and autographed it for me... I was manager at the time Allen Ginsberg did a reading and afterwards we all went over to the Spring Street Bar expecting to hear stories about wild sex and famous beats. But all Allen wanted to talk about was how much money he made per book. I got drunk and wandered away, bitterly disappointed."

THE BOOKWORM

CHINA
2002 TO PRESENT

The Bookworm is a popular library, bar, restaurant, and event space with five locations in Beijing, Suzhou, and Chengdu. It has been recognized as one of the world's best bookshops by Lonely Planet and since 2006 has hosted the China Bookworm Literary Festival featuring artists, writers, performers, and thinkers. In 2015 it founded the China Bookworm Press, an independent publisher of leading contemporary fiction and nonfiction in China, in Chinese and other languages. The Bookworm also publishes a literary journal, *MaLa*, supporting Chinese culture.

During his campaign,
President Obama phoned in and fielded questions
over the speakers from a packed Bookworm bookstore.

"At our monthly Basically Beethoven classical music open mic,
someone roamed in with a tuba and went on to play an entire concerto."
—Anthony Tao, The Bookworm

HATCHARDS

LONDON, ENGLAND
1797 TO PRESENT

———

Hatchards of Piccadilly is England's most aristocratic shop in Britain and the bookstore of Her Majesty the Queen. It has been selling books in the same building for over two centuries. Shoppers have included former prime minister Benjamin Disraeli, Oscar Wilde, and Lord Byron.

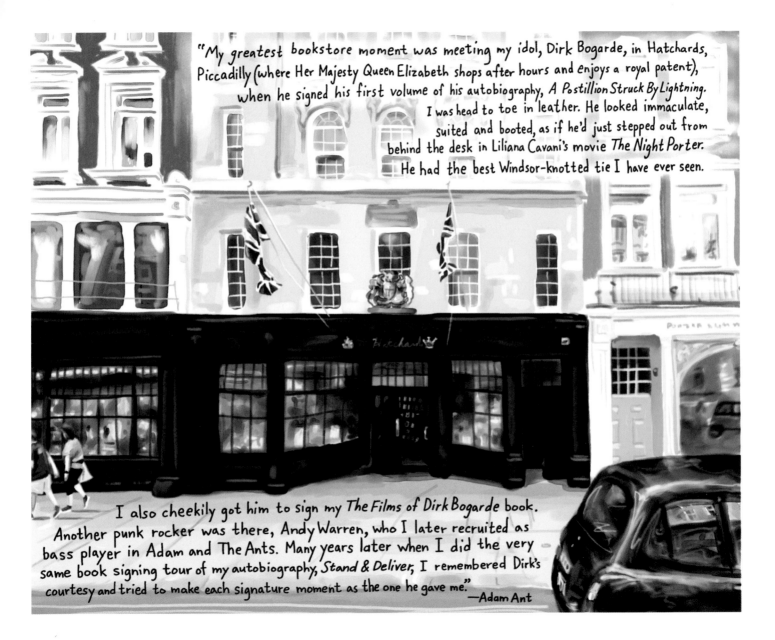

"My greatest bookstore moment was meeting my idol, Dirk Bogarde, in Hatchards, Piccadilly (where Her Majesty Queen Elizabeth shops after hours and enjoys a royal patent), when he signed his first volume of his autobiography, *A Postillion Struck By Lightning*. I was head to toe in leather. He looked immaculate, suited and booted, as if he'd just stepped out from behind the desk in Liliana Cavani's movie *The Night Porter*. He had the best Windsor-knotted tie I have ever seen.

I also cheekily got him to sign my *The Films of Dirk Bogarde* book. Another punk rocker was there, Andy Warren, who I later recruited as bass player in Adam and The Ants. Many years later when I did the very same book signing tour of my autobiography, *Stand & Deliver*, I remembered Dirk's courtesy and tried to make each signature moment as the one he gave me."

—Adam Ant

MCNALLY JACKSON

NEW YORK CITY
2004 TO PRESENT

———

McNally Jackson is one of the largest independent bookstores in Manhattan at 7,000 square feet.

"Lou Reed asked for a quarter for the lock on the bathroom door. He was wondering why there was a coin lock there at all, and a staffer explained it was because of problems with junkies flushing needles down the toilet. 'You wouldn't believe what people will flush down the toilet,' the staffer said. 'Trust me,' Lou replied, 'I would.'" —Sarah McNally, owner

GIOVANNI'S ROOM

PHILADELPHIA, PENNSYLVANIA
1973 TO PRESENT

Giovanni's Room is the longest-running gay bookstore in the United States. Former owners Ed Hermance and Arleen Olshan purchased the building that housed the store in 1979 and more than one hundred people volunteered to help renovate the building. From the 1980s to the mid-1990s, Giovanni's was America's biggest distributor of gay publishing, serving eighty-eight stores in seventeen different countries.

Ed Hermance explained that at the end the store could not sustain solely as a bookstore: "It was not profitable . . . but an awful lot of fun. . . . If there was ever a community bookstore, this is it. The gay community created this bookstore for itself." Hermance retired in 2014, and the bookstore was taken over by Philly AIDS Thrift at Giovanni's Room, a nonprofit where 100 percent of the proceeds goes to HIV Aids organizations.

One of Hermance's most memorable sales was a copy of a book titled *Lesbian Nuns* to the Vatican Library.

"For the first fifteen years, occasionally we would get busted windows, and it always struck me that these broken windows always happened in the dead of night," remembers Hermance. "Similar things would happen when people stopped at the traffic light at the corner. When the light turned green, they would squeal off shouting, 'Faggots!' at the top of their lungs, and you'd think, who's the sissy here? Those throwing bricks at three in the morning and screaming as they're driving away. Is this the worst they can do to us?"

RICHARD BOOTH'S BOOKSHOP

HAY-ON-WYE, WALES
1961 TO PRESENT

Richard Booth's Bookshop began in 1961 when Booth bought buildings in Hay-on-Wye, Wales—including the hamlet's Main Street shops, its old fire station, the cinema, a Victorian workhouse, and the crumbling Norman Castle—and turned them into used bookstores. The Oxford graduate started the "Booktown Movement." By the 1970s, Hay-on-Wye had a million books and thirty-eight secondhand bookshops and was known worldwide as the "Town of Books." There are now over sixty towns around the world, from South Korea to Stillwater, Minnesota. Today Hay-on-Wye contains around a dozen stores, and Richard Booth sold his Richard Booth's Bookshop in 2005, now Europe's largest secondhand bookshop, and opened a new shop in town called the King of Hay. Every June the Hay Literary Festival attracts tens of thousands of visitors and some of the biggest literary names from around the world.

Richard Booth recruited Hay's strongest men and went to America's closing libraries and shipped back freight containers of books on his way to becoming the world's largest secondhand book dealer. In 1977 Richard Booth proclaimed himself King and Hay an independent kingdom. As King Richard Cœur de Livre, he named his horse as the prime minister. Richard Booth was awarded an MBE in 2004. In 2009 he was "beheaded" by the residents of Hay in good fun. The "revolting peasants" used a stuffed body double.

Throughout Hay-on-Wye, there are honesty boxes to leave payment for books available on the al fresco bookcases.

ANTHONY FROST ENGLISH BOOKSHOP

BUCHAREST, ROMANIA
2007 TO 2017

———————

The Anthony Frost English Bookshop was opened by three friends with a fascination for the English language. It is the second oldest all-English bookshop in Bucharest, Romania (the first is Nautilus, which opened in 1998).

FOR RENT
Suprafata 4000 m
Tel: 0721 85394

"A young couple's first encounter was by chance when both tried to purchase the same book. But there was just one copy. They came back after some years, married."
—Vlad Niculescu, owner

HUMANITAS

ANTHONY FROST

librarias J MANITAS

menu Cafe

"On a day off from teaching, I came across this bookshop. I chatted for an hour with Vlad, the warm and affable owner, and spent three times what I'd intended. Most of the books had to be shipped back to the States (too heavy!). As I left the shop, I noticed a spray-painted bit of prose.

SPIT HERE IF YOU THINK LIFE IS BEAUTIFUL

—Harry Bliss, New Yorker cartoonist

BART'S BOOKS

OJAI, CALIFORNIA
1964 TO PRESENT

The largest outdoor independent bookstore in America is at the corner of Matilija and Canada Street in the city of Ojai, California. Bart's Books started when a personal book collection grew so massive that bookcases were placed outside along the sidewalk with coffee cans for shoppers to leave money. Since that time, the 1960s home turned into a bookshop with all levels of books, including rare, out-of-print first editions and art books valued in the thousands of dollars. Its two garages and a large patio are jammed with bookshelves containing more than 100,000 used books, and for books outside, the honor system is still in use.

The bookshop began having a sign-in guest book after Paul Newman and Joanne Woodward dropped by looking for an old edition of *Huck Finn*.

The subject of numerous TV documentaries, Bart's was once secretly filmed from a van across the street to see how honest people were and if people would pay for books when no one was around. People came by in cars, by bicycle, on horseback, or on foot to buy books after hours. It was a rare occurrence for a visitor to take a book without paying. Gary Schlicter, one of the former owners, says nighttime shoppers "often used vehicle headlights or flashlights to help read the titles and browse."

192 BOOKS

NEW YORK CITY
2003 TO PRESENT

---

192 Books opened in 2003 in Chelsea at 192 Tenth Avenue in New York City. It is owned and "curated" by art dealer Paula Cooper.

For the hundredth
anniversary of Proust's *Swann's Way*,
the store hosted a 24-hour reading of the book. The *New Yorker's*
Adam Gopnik and biographer Anka Muhlstein made the introductions.
   The first lines were read by poet/critic Wayne Koestenbaum. At midnight, five
hours in, Ethan Hawke wandered in, still in theater makeup from a performance
of *Clive*, to take a turn reading. Other readers included Michael Cunningham and
Laurie Anderson. Two patrons stayed and listened to the entire 24-hour reading.

BARBARA'S BOOKSTORE

CHICAGO, ILLINOIS
1963 TO PRESENT

Started by a woman named Barbara, who after two or so years had nothing to do with the chain, Barbara's Bookstore is a cluster of stores in Chicago with one satellite location in Boston. At one time Barbara's Booksstore also had shops in Philadelphia, New York, and Minneapolis.

The Barbara's Bookstore in the Willis Tower is located in the basement. Its two comfy chairs are sometimes a refuge for those scared of heights as the rest of their party ascend to the tower's Sky Deck. Once, an old man was so still for so long that the store manager (ex-comedian Rick Kotrba) slammed a neighboring door, afraid he had passed on (he was pleased to see the old man jump). Kotrba's philosophy is singular: "Booksellers are on a mission from God, and depending upon how inspired they may be feeling on any given day, they are liable to provide a particular tier of service ranging from healing everybody who walks in the door to merely amusing them to just selling them books."

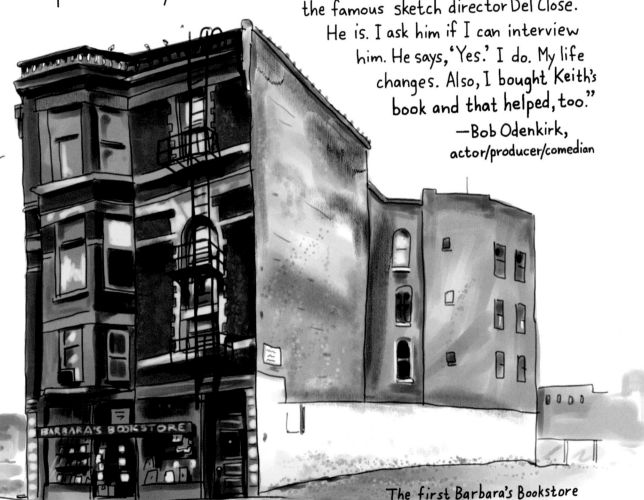

"February 1983: a 21-year-old me is in Barbara's Bookstore on Wells Street flipping through Keith Johnstone's seminal improvisation book *Impro*. A scruffy fellow enters and chats it up with the lady clerk. She calls him 'Del.' I find a moment to ask if he's the famous sketch director Del Close. He is. I ask him if I can interview him. He says, 'Yes.' I do. My life changes. Also, I bought Keith's book and that helped, too."

—Bob Odenkirk,
actor/producer/comedian

The first Barbara's Bookstore on Wells Street in Chicago's Old Town neighborhood.

Recollections
from Rick Kotrba,
manager of Barbara's
Bookstore:

"A middle-aged woman asked for a book on dinosaurs.
I showed her one and her response was,
'Well, these illustrations are nice but are just
drawings. I want one with real photographs.'
I didn't know how to break it to her that
the camera wasn't invented for another
zillion years."

"One customer necessitated the store later
post a sign YOU LICK IT, YOU BUY IT."

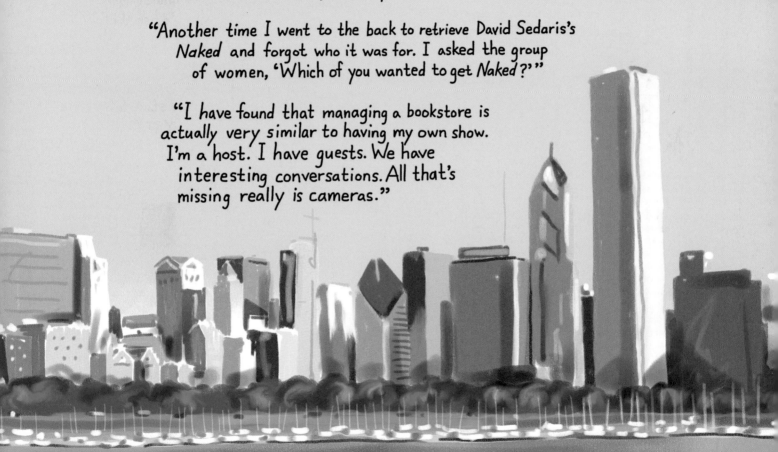

"A woman was looking to buy Alice Khan Lada's best seller, *The G Spot*. I went in the back and came back proudly announcing, 'Ma'am, I found your G-spot!'"

"Another time I went to the back to retrieve David Sedaris's *Naked* and forgot who it was for. I asked the group of women, 'Which of you wanted to get *Naked*?'"

"I have found that managing a bookstore is actually very similar to having my own show. I'm a host. I have guests. We have interesting conversations. All that's missing really is cameras."

bob

MUNRO'S BOOKS

VANCOUVER ISLAND, CANADA
1963 TO PRESENT

———

Munro's Books' latest location is housed in a beautiful heritage-award-winning 1909 neoclassical building originally designed for the Royal Bank of Canada by Thomas Hooper.

In 1963, Jim and Alice Munro opened a small narrow shop of paperbacks. Jim says his then-wife, Alice, while working some shifts in the store, was inspired to write: "One day she got mad and she said, 'I can write better books than this.' She could. There's no question." The Munros themselves would go their own way in 1972, and Alice Munro would go on to win the 2013 Nobel Prize in Literature and the Man Booker Prize. After over fifty years as owner, Jim Munro retired in 2014 and handed the store over to four of his employees.

"We had a crow fly into the store and take up residence once. This development was covered by the local newspaper, which helped business as many people came to see the crow. We tried to tempt it with food, large ladders were employed, animal control and a bird specialist came to look, but the crow could not be persuaded to come down—our ceilings are approximately twenty -four feet high.

Eventually it got exhausted and let itself be caught." —Jessica Walker, majority owner

FAULKNER HOUSE BOOKS

NEW ORLEANS, LOUISIANA
1990 TO PRESENT

———————

Faulkner House Books of New Orleans, Louisiana, is also responsible for the annual Faulkner Society's festival, Words & Music, as well as an international literary competition, The William Faulkner-Wisdom Creative Writing Competition, both of which are nonprofit.

Mississippian William Faulkner wrote *Soldier's Pay* at 624 Pirate's Alley, where he once lived and is now the location of Faulkner House Books.

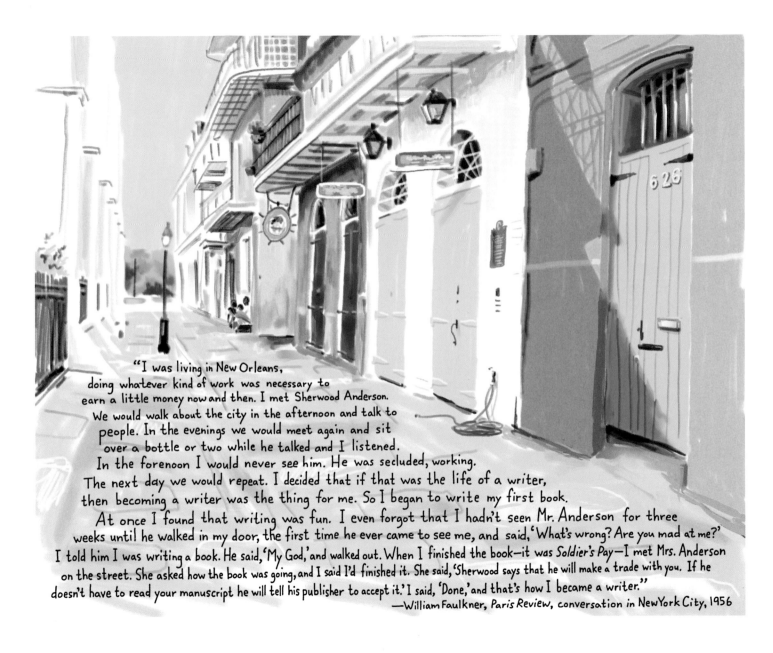

"I was living in New Orleans,
doing whatever kind of work was necessary to
earn a little money now and then. I met Sherwood Anderson.
We would walk about the city in the afternoon and talk to
people. In the evenings we would meet again and sit
over a bottle or two while he talked and I listened.
In the forenoon I would never see him. He was secluded, working.
The next day we would repeat. I decided that if that was the life of a writer,
then becoming a writer was the thing for me. So I began to write my first book.
At once I found that writing was fun. I even forgot that I hadn't seen Mr. Anderson for three
weeks until he walked in my door, the first time he ever came to see me, and said, 'What's wrong? Are you mad at me?'
I told him I was writing a book. He said, 'My God,' and walked out. When I finished the book—it was *Soldier's Pay*—I met Mrs. Anderson
on the street. She asked how the book was going, and I said I'd finished it. She said, 'Sherwood says that he will make a trade with you. If he
doesn't have to read your manuscript he will tell his publisher to accept it.' I said, 'Done,' and that's how I became a writer."
—William Faulkner, *Paris Review*, conversation in New York City, 1956

DAEDALUS BOOKSHOP

CHARLOTTESVILLE, VIRGINIA
1975 TO PRESENT

The owner of Daedalus Bookshop, Sandy McAdams, previously ran a bookstore in a barn in Westhampton on New York's Long Island. In 1974, someone—unprompted by him—sent him a photo of a building for sale in Charlottesville, Virginia. He liked what he saw, so he loaded all his books in a freight car and headed for Virginia and never looked back. Daedalus Bookshop now has over 100,000 used books.

In 2001 Sandy was diagnosed with MS. Today he gets around in a motorized wheelchair. "There may be one or two other bookstores like this, but not many, and they're going out of business. If I didn't own the building, we would be gone."

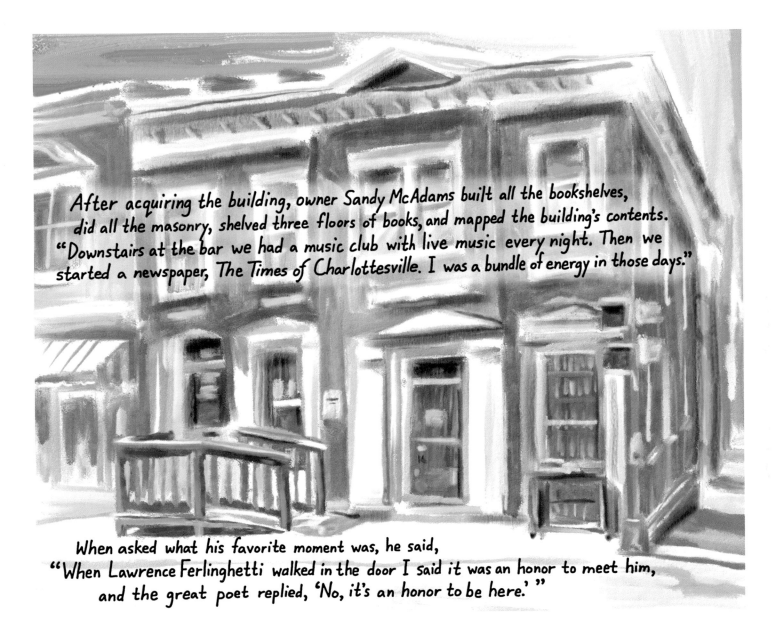

After acquiring the building, owner Sandy McAdams built all the bookshelves, did all the masonry, shelved three floors of books, and mapped the building's contents. "Downstairs at the bar we had a music club with live music every night. Then we started a newspaper, *The Times of Charlottesville*. I was a bundle of energy in those days."

When asked what his favorite moment was, he said, "When Lawrence Ferlinghetti walked in the door I said it was an honor to meet him, and the great poet replied, 'No, it's an honor to be here.'"

THE WATERMILL BOOKSHOP

ABERFELDY, SCOTLAND
2005 TO PRESENT

The Watermill Bookshop is housed in a former watermill in Aberfeldy in the Perthshire Highlands of Scotland and has the largest range of titles in the Scottish Highlands. At the 2009 Bookseller Retail Awards, it was selected the UK Independent Bookshop of the Year.

When asked for his
most memorable bookstore moment,
Monty Python's Michael Palin said it was the time
he opened the Watermill Bookshop in the Scottish countryside:
"The most perfect conjunction. The owner of my favourite local bookshop in Kentish Town, London, decamps
to the most beautiful countryside in Scotland and decides to turn an old mill into a bookstore.
  I'm asked to open it, and witness Kevin, the owner, flinging himself on the waterwheel to get started.
  I expect it to be a magnificent failure, but it's been a magnificent success. Walter Scott is no longer
        the only reason for book-lovers to go to Scotland."

LIBRERIA ACQUA ALTA

VENICE, ITALY
2005 TO PRESENT

————————

Libreria Acqua Alta ("Library of High Water") is located in Calle Lunga Santa Maria Formosa with its door spilling out onto the local canal. It sells posters, postcards, objects of art, and thousands of both used and new books in multiple languages. It calls itself the "most beautiful bookstore in the world," and this would be hard to argue. Due to Venice's constant flooding, most of the used and new books were shelved in, sometimes floating, bathtubs, barrels, canoes, and a huge gondola inside the store.

During a flood in February of 2015, shoppers browsed the store in two feet of water. Many of the waterlogged books, like enormous old encyclopedias, are no longer for sale but have been repurposed as furniture, walls, and even the steps to a unique staircase.

"There was an erotica section just as you walk in...could've done without that."
—anonymous customer

FIRESIDE BOOKS

PALMER, ALASKA
2001 TO PRESENT

Located in the small agricultural town of Palmer, Alaska, Fireside Books was founded as an excuse to hold poetry readings. It is now a full-service bookstore selling both new and used books.

"In the fall of 2001, a sign appeared in a storefront in Palmer, Alaska:
BOOKSTORE COMING SOON
Whenever I drove by, I would slow down and try to peek in the windows, and over weeks I watched boxes being stacked and unpacked and bare wooden shelves installed. I can't remember ever being so excited about something in my hometown. But as much as I anticipated its opening, I never could have imagined how this little bookstore would change my fate. Owners David Cheezem and Melissa Behnke were among the first to read *The Snow Child* when it was still an unpublished manuscript. In February 2012, they hosted my book release party. Since then they have surely sold the most copies of *The Snow Child* of any single bookstore in the world. David openly jokes that *The Snow Child* financially saved Fireside Books last year. I hope it is true. It would barely scratch the surface of my debt to them."

—Eowyn Ivey, bestselling author and
2013 PNBA Award recipient, author of *The Snow Child*

UN REGARD MODERNE

PARIS, FRANCE
MID-1980S TO PRESENT

Un Regard Moderne houses thousands of volumes—mostly art and pop culture—in two crowded rooms that only four to five people can fit into at a time. Affectionately considered by many to be the greatest bookstore on earth, customers have ranged from William S. Burroughs to Sonic Youth.

"Un Regard Moderne is the cathedral of international counterculture."

—Atlas Obscura

"It's easy to walk past it. Even now, knowing exactly where to find it, I don't 'see' it unless I'm really, really looking for it. The last time I stepped in was 2007, and there was only room for one person in the passages. My work had gained a lot of attention by that time and *Juxtapoz* had done a nice feature on me, and there was a copy of the magazine right on one of the stacks. For me, this was something I never could have imagined! It was like a personal dream come true to be *inside* this bookstore in that way. It's like a holy site and you feel anointed!"
—Jenny Hart, artist

"It is the strangest fucking place I've ever been in. You don't see it until there it is. When I spoke to the famous owner, Jacques Noel, and started to explain about your book, he immediately went ice cold and said, 'Je n'existe plus' (I'm no longer here). Why he no longer existed, I do not know." —Allen Stone, writer

GREENLIGHT BOOKSTORE

BROOKLYN, NEW YORK
2007 TO PRESENT

———

Greenlight Bookstore began in 2007 out of community demand in the Brooklyn neighborhood of Fort Greene and thanks to a $15,000 grand prize from a local business-plan competition. In 2014 the Greenlight Bookstore Radio Hour was started, and in 2016 they opened a second shop, in the Prospect-Lefferts Gardens neighborhood of Brooklyn.

"One day a young woman asked us which Jennifer Egan book she should read, while holding up two. We recommended Look At Me and then suggested 'If you'd like it signed, Jennifer Egan is right next to you and is quite nice.'
    A woman at the register told one of our booksellers, 'Five years ago I bought all my books online, but now I'm just sort of over it.'"

—Rebecca Fitting, Greenlight Bookstore

LITERATI BOOKSHOP

GOA, INDIA
2006 TO PRESENT

Located in a one-hundred-year-old home in a garden in Goa, India, is the Literati Bookshop and café. Outside art exhibits, film screenings, Italian potluck dinners, photography shows, and author readings move indoors during the monsoons. Owner Diviya Kapur stopped being a lawyer in Delhi to fulfill her dream of owning a bookshop with a café. Literati was selected Bookstore of the Year 2014, Publishing Next Industry Award. It is now involved with Bebook, a mobile library for disadvantaged children.

"It is a respite. Inside the cool, high-ceiling room, they order you a lime soda from across the road while you sit amidst the pile of books you've chosen. I was doing just that when someone leaned over the sofa and asked the age-old question, 'Don't I know you?' In a few leaps and bends we got there. Party in the 1990s, NYC."

—Ilene Antelman, customer

"The secret of Literati is that it's much more than a bookshop. To say that it's a home away from home doesn't quite do it justice either, because it's always full of surprises—if you're lucky you may even see a snake slipping by." —Amitav Ghosh, *The Glass Palace*

THE LAST BOOKSTORE

LOS ANGELES, CALIFORNIA
2005 TO PRESENT

The Last Bookstore is one of the largest independent bookstores in the world, with over 250,000 new, used, and rare books in its collection, including a back room of 100,000 books that sell for $1. The tunnel to the room was made solely with $1 books. The space was originally a bank, and its underground vaults are now reading rooms.

"I was at the Last Bookstore, wandering through its vast labyrinth of bookcases, book tunnels, book archways, book pillars, and revolving books to nowhere.

It was like experiencing temporary insanity, from which I hoped I would never recover.

'A good book is more precious than a safe filled with rare coins and uncut gems,' someone said, just before I woke up." —Joe Frank, radio artist

ENDNOTES AND MISCELLANY

1. *"Many years ago, Patty Marx, Jane Martin, and I were doing a book event at a bookstore for Now Everybody Really Hates Me, a children's book we collaborated on. During the Q&A, a weird-looking lady stood up, pointed at all of us, and said, 'I can tell that none of you believe in god. Also, you are all ugly.' The bookstore people scooted her out. I guess she was a well-known bag lady who often showed up at events, but somehow she'd slipped under the radar."*

   —ROZ CHAST, *New Yorker* cartoonist, author of *Can't We Talk About Something More Pleasant?*

2. *"That woman was sitting in the front row and wearing a parka. It was August. To promote that same book [Now Everybody Really Hates Me], Jane and I went to an elementary school in Boston, where a kid asked us the best question I've ever been asked: 'How many inches apart do you two live from each other?' Another kid, finding out we lived in New York, asked if we knew his grandmother who also lived in New York. We did not. He then asked if we knew the Sterns. We did not. Finally, he asked, 'Do you know anyone?'"*

   —PATRICIA MARX, humorist, author of *Let's Be Less Stupid*

3. *"Patti Smith briefly worked with me at the Strand in the seventies. At a SoHo rooftop reading she did for Arthur Rimbaud's birthday, someone gave her a vinyl LP of James Joyce reading Finnegans Wake, 'because they told me I looked like James Joyce.' She brought it back to the store and gave it to me because she knew I liked Joyce, 'and because I don't look like him at all. That's bullshit. You keep it.'"*

   —RON KOLM, poet

4. *"When we announced that Jo Nesbø was coming to Bratislava, the response was as if he were a rock star. His fans went crazy, and the media coverage couldn't have been higher. We called in crowd-management and security professionals to determine the maximum capacity of our bookstore, and it was set around five hundred people. To make things fair we released tickets in several waves online; however, full capacity was reached in seventy-seven seconds. We had never met Mr. Nesbø in person before, so after all this frenzy I wouldn't have been surprised if he had some real attitude, but he turned out to be very nice, tirelessly answering any questions and giving autographs and smiles for pictures. He is a huge FC Barcelona fan, and his team was playing in the Champions League semifinals that very day, so we set up a live screening of the match in the store, with his fans, and he watched his team beat Bayern Munich 3-0 and make it to the finals."*

   —MICHAL BRAT, manager of Martinus Bookstore

5. *"The proprietor of Shakespeare, an insanely remarkable guy named George Whitman, who died at ninety-eight or something, would let aspiring writers spend the night there in exchange for working the desk. You would camp out on beds and couches sprinkled around the store after the store closed at midnight. One morning I woke up and found that the other person in my bed was my college roommate's girlfriend."*

   —DAVID S. ROSE, book collector

6. *"One of our famous characters that regularly held court at Adobe was Red Man, a.k.a. Prince Charm. He painted his face and exposed body parts red every day and had the strangest worldview I have ever heard. We had a show for him where artists painted his portrait."*

   —CHRISTINE SHIELDS, manager

7. *"My most memorable bookstore moment happened at Books & Books in Coral Gables, which is a wonderful store. My coauthor, Ridley Pearson, and I were reading a passage from Peter and the Secret of Rundoon to a roomful of kids. This particular passage involved a huge man-eating snake. Unbeknownst to Ridley and me, the bookstore owner, Mitchell Kaplan, had decided to liven things up by arranging to have a man bring in a ninety-pound, ten-foot-long albino Burmese python, which the man proceeded to drape across our shoulders. As the snake*

coiled around us, we tried to keep reading, pretending that we were enjoying ourselves. We were not enjoying ourselves. We were wishing we had brought along some spare underwear."

—DAVE BARRY

---

8. "I was to give a reading at BookCourt, my local bookstore, and I wanted to do something different. I contacted this woman, a circus performer. One of her things is to lie on a bed of nails with a cinder block on her belly, which then gets smashed with a sledgehammer. We had worked together before. I had used the sledgehammer. But she wasn't available. She suggested Throwdini, a knife thrower, who is also a part-time rabbi. So he came to BookCourt and in front of about two hundred people—store was packed—he threw knives at me and I trusted him. I don't know why. But I survived. I kept my eyes closed and prayed to God, even though I'm agnostic. Two years later, in 2011, I re-created that scene for the TV show I was writing at the time, which was quasi-autobiographical. The actor playing Jonathan Ames had knives thrown at him by Throwdini in BookCourt. This time the knives were fake."

—JONATHAN AMES

9. "For one event, only a small number showed up at the bookstore, so I just took the group out to dinner."

—BOB MANKOFF, *New Yorker* cartoon editor, author of *How About Never—Is Never Good for You?: My Life in Cartoons*

---

10. "I have been at work on this narrative nonfiction for a long time. The events of it take place in interwar Hungary in a remote village on the Great Plains. One night I had this dream, an exhausting dream, that I was driving all over Budapest and other parts of Hungary looking for something, but I didn't know what. The following day I drove my friend to Bratislava, Slovakia. While he was at his appointment, I went to a new bookstore called Martinus (new to me, anyway). I headed to the English-language section, which is always very limited and usually full of Penguin Classics. Not this time. The first book I saw was a translation of Gyula Krúdy's Life Is a Dream. Krúdy will mean nothing to you, but he is one of Hungary's most celebrated writers (and a gorgeous writer). It was as if all that driving in my dream the evening before had actually led me somewhere. Krúdy wrote during the interwar period and about village life. It was the only book the store had by Krúdy in English—and a single copy at that. It somehow felt like a sign that I was, perhaps, heading in the right direction, even if I did feel like I was driving all over the place."

—PATTI MCCRACKEN

11. "Before I was a manager at Barbara's, I worked as a clerk at a chain. Harry Potter #7 was coming out, and soon the store would be teeming with humanity. The boxes in the back had large red warning labels not to open before the next morning. My manager was a huge fan and directed me to open a box—she did not read the book in advance but explained she could not wait until tomorrow to see if Harry lived or died. So I quickly skimmed the later portions of the book and arrived at "All is well." He is fine, I told my boss, and she exhaled. Riding the Metro that night I had the surreal thought that I'm the only person in Chicago who knew if Harry lives or dies."

—RICK KOTRBA

---

12. "A hooker approached me and asked if I wanted to make $20—there's a twist. All I had to do was show up at a party and act artsy. Plus all the potato chips and beer I could consume. At that party the folk singer they hired was great. In the elevator leaving the party I told him, 'You got something special.' Two years later I recognized the face on the cover of a record album in the window of the bookstore—Bob Dylan."

—ARNIE LEVIN, professional Beatnik and *New Yorker* cartoonist

13. *"Traveler Restaurant was the first bookstore I did and unknowingly set the tone for the rest of the book. I had a long conversation with its owners and spent far longer on the painting than I expected. I've been there many times and I will share that (1) the better books are downstairs, which you have to pay for, and (2) you will not be disappointed if you go with the cod and clams."*

—BOB ECKSTEIN

---

14. *"I drove my mother and sister, who were visiting from London, to the Hamptons, as they had heard many stories about it being the place 'to be and be seen.' Having coffee on Main Street we ran into a lady called Jenny. She asked if I remembered a conversation we had a couple of years earlier about a book she intended to write, a parody on the best-selling book The Rules. She did publish this book, Get a Life, Then Get a Man. She took an instant liking to Mom and said she would love to get her a copy (I'm not sure why, as my mother was and still is happily married). We agreed to go into the bookstore, which was a couple of doors away. As we were standing around, while Jenny went to grab some copies, I saw a 'Vision in White' enter. I told my mom not to look around but that Tom Wolfe just walked in. Both my mom and I are huge fans since The Bonfire of the Vanities. Of course, she instantly turned right around. When Jenny came back, Mom couldn't tell her fast enough. Jenny says, 'Tom Wolfe? I know him,' and then walks over to him a few feet away and says, 'Tom, hello, it's Jenny.*

We met at a cocktail party at so-and-so's . . .' Mom and I watched in fascination and fell more in love with Mr. Wolfe, who obviously hadn't a clue who this woman was but said, 'Ah, Jenny, of course, so nice to see you again.' She then said, 'I've just written a book,' and shoves one into his hands, calls my mother over, and hands her a copy, too. She points toward the cashier's desk and says the words I will never forget: 'Tom . . . Marie . . . just head over there to pay for them.' Mr. Wolfe, being the true southern gentleman that he is, thanks her and walks over to pay with my mom following suit. A few minutes later, Jenny runs over and says to both, 'Here, let me sign these for you.' But at this point Mom is in seventh heaven and tells me that she can die a happy woman having had the chance to stand next to Tom Wolfe in Bookhampton, exchanging smiles with each other that neither of them would ever read this book."

—TINA SIMMS, customer, Bookhampton

---

15. *"I just want to tell you about our concert at Zweitausendeins,"* says Aline Kominsky-Crumb, who performed a jazz show at the Hamburg bookstore in 2003 with her husband (cartoonist Robert Crumb) and their daughter. *"It was a total nightmare! I didn't practice enough, and I am not a professional musician. The German audience just pressed up close to us and looked at us like laboratory animals. I was completely paralyzed, and my daughter, Sophie, was obliged to cover up for my total failure. When I got home, I gave my violin away, and I have never played publicly since then and I will never do that again in this lifetime! I love to listen to great music, and my husband and daughter are both great performers and I admire them both."*

---

16. *"If you do not send them to me, to round out my little edition of Stevenson [newly published letters], I will haunt you in the shape of a rattlesnake with the voice of a tiger, and I will steadily, for the next 18 years, put spiders in your tea!! So there!!! Respectfully yours, Royal Cortissoz"*

—ART CRITIC, *New York Tribune*, writing to Ray Safford, Scribner's retail chief, June 13, 1911

---

17. *"I love the idea of the project you're doing and would certainly love to be a part of it. Here's my dirty secret. I almost never go into bookstores. We get crates of books in the mail every day. I'm surrounded by books in my office, at home, in the studio. Books, books, books. Everywhere. So I don't go to bookstores hunting for more books. I also don't have time to read books that I'm not reading for the show. Because I'm always reading for the show. When I do walk into a bookstore, I just feel guilty, as if the books are crying out to me: 'Interview my author! She'd make a great guest and more people would want to buy me.' "*

—NPR'S TERRY GROSS

18. "When I was around twelve or thirteen I would go to the B. Dalton bookstore in Albuquerque, New Mexico, at the Winrock Shopping Center . . . named after Winthrop Rockefeller. I would go in there to the humor section where they had a book called A History of Underground Comics [by Mark James Estren, PhD], and in that book there's a panel by Estren with two people floating in space like a constellation and they're having sex, so they're connected sexually. And I don't think I'd ever seen it before that, how everything sort of fit together, and it was that book, in that bookstore. I would visit that book fairly frequently because there was a lot of sex in there, and I would just sit there in the aisle with a boner in B. Dalton bookstore, doing everything short of masturbating and learning about sex."

—MARC MARON

19. Morrissey was browsing alone in the Strand when an old woman suddenly fell. He picked up her stray belongings and asked if he could get her some water or call for help. She collected her things and before leaving touched Morrissey's cheek in gratitude, unaware who this nice British man was.

20. "Keeping one step ahead of the military, I bolted for San Francisco, where I dosed myself with LSD, had my psychiatric record confirmed by the doctor who treated me at the hospital, and was termed too crazy to serve. . . . When I got to San Francisco—it was June 1966—I looked up a college friend who was working at City Lights. City Lights had the atmosphere of a funky Left Bank cave with flimsy cellar bookshelves partly made of orange crates, some rickety café tables, and chairs for reading. To be a clerk at City Lights was a more intimate privilege. The dissident poet-publisher who owned the store, Lawrence Ferlinghetti, still took an occasional turn at the register."

—JAN HERMAN, editor, publisher, author of *My Adventures in Fugitive Literature*

21. "When I first came to New York in 1988, used book stores were my haunts. I didn't go to clubs, bars, or restaurants. I couldn't afford them. Used bookstores charged no entrance fee. And they were full of the romance of the city's literary and cultural past. . . . The Strand was the most famous, and the biggest. But too big for me. You could get lost in it, but not necessarily lost in it. I preferred the Rare Book Room on the second floor, which took me a year or so to find out about. It had a separate entrance and was reached by an elevator. The prizes were up there, as well as an intimacy and a quietude. . . . With the onslaught of Barnes & Noble in the early '90s, many independent bookstores closed. The most heartbreaking shuttering to me was the New York City Bookstore at Rockefeller Center. This was a one-of-a-kind bookstore, never seen before and never to be seen again. It carried only books about New York City. It was the most romantic New York bookstore to my mind. I would drool over first editions of WPA guides to New York and studies of the city by E. B. White, Joseph Mitchell, and the like. People seem to have completely forgotten about this bookstore. It was magical. Pure unadulterated New York-iana. There is a J. Crew where it used to be. I remember around this time coming up with an idea of a kind of coffee table book about all the important vanished bookstores of New York City, the historical ones dating back to the early 1900s on. I was very enthusiastic about the idea. I suggested it to a friend, a fellow journalist. He dismissed it as worthy of maybe a long article, not a book. I remember being so angry with him that I really didn't want to know him anymore. I never did see him again."

—ROBERT SIMONSON, *Lost City* creator and *New York Times* writer

22. "The Gotham Book Mart had an art gallery on the second floor, and I used to eat my lunchtime sandwiches up there on a little round table set in the back. One day Andy [Brown] came in from his morning up at Sotheby's auction house. He came over to me and looked at my lunch and told me to go wash my hands, he had a treat to show me. It was the handwritten manuscript of D. H. Lawrence's unpublished novel Mr. Noon. My hands passed inspection, and I opened the notebook to clear, neat, and very small peacock blue ink: D. H. Lawrence's final draft of Mr. Noon. Andy bought the notebook for a client of his, and I remember that it wasn't published for another ten years—by which time I had my own bookstore and I ordered copies of the book and I never sold a single copy, but it was still my honor to carry such a book."

—MATTHEW TANNENBAUM

---

23. "During the Q&A at a reading by a prominent fiction writer, a man stood in the back row and said: 'I'm a heart surgeon and I'm about to retire. I'd like to write a novel. Do you have any tips for me?' Without hesitation, the writer retorted: 'What a coincidence! I'm about to write my last novel and thought I'd try my hand at heart surgery. Any ideas?'"

—MITCHELL KAPLAN, owner of Books & Books

---

24. "I had a happy surprise the other day when I was passing down East Fourth Street. A small storefront with prints displayed on the sidewalk bore a sign reading PAGEANT, the letters painted a familiar shade of blue. Could it be? It was. After five years selling over the Internet, the shop—now exclusively prints, no books—had reopened. I was delighted to see it again and skipped right in. Almost immediately upon entering, however, I remembered why I had never frequented Pageant as much as other used-books stores. I addressed the woman with long, dark red, curly hair behind the counter—recognizable as the owner from the old days. Was this the same Pageant? She waited, unsmiling, for me to stumble through my question, which

needn't have been as long and drawn-out as it was if she had just nodded her head or something. She eventually grunted a yes. 'How long have you been here?' I asked. 'I got here about 10:30 a.m.,' she answered. Comedienne. 'I mean, when did the store open here?' 'About a year and a half ago.' Still no smile. Trying to remain upbeat, I said, 'Well, I'm glad I found you again.' 'I didn't know I was lost,' she drawled. This I remembered. At East Ninth Street, Pageant always had the surliest, most sarcastic service in the New York book world."

—ROBERT SIMONSON, *Lost City* creator and *New York Times* writer

---

25. "Carly Simon actually wanted to sell me her copy of Jackie Robinson's biography in which his widow personally signed and thanked the Simon publishing family for putting his family up in their Connecticut home during the summer of 1955 for a year and a half at a time when others wouldn't."

—DISTINGUISHED BOOKSELLER

---

26. "When I was young I worked for Frances Steloff of Gotham Book Mart. The first time she saw me wrapping books she said, "You have no beauty in you!" She subsequently changed her opinion. She and I went to readings at the 92nd Street Y to sell books, often accompanied in the taxi by poet Marianne Moore. I also delivered books to Allen Ginsberg. Yes, sometimes he came to the door

naked. One time someone who was in the store asked to come along. He was rather 'creepy' (I was eighteen). It turned out to be John Wieners, author of The Hotel Wentley Poems, a writer I adored at the time."

—PROFESSOR HENRY WEINFELD, University of Notre Dame

---

27. "For ten years or so, John Grisham did a book signing every year. Sometime in the early 1990s, before we began limiting the number of people who could attend, the line stretched out the door and down the block. Midpoint during the event we received a phone call from a man asking if books were still available—he was at the end of the line and calling from the pay phone a block away. Mr. Grisham got up from his seat and headed out the door with a copy for the gentleman."

—COREY MESLER, owner of Burke's Book Store

---

28. "I spent a good four years in the early '90s scouring the nooks and crannies of every used bookstore between South Carolina and New Hampshire for old copies of Steve Martin's Cruel Shoes. I probably bought forty or more copies over the years and gave them out to everyone I knew. Mainly because I thought it was the best thing ever but also because it felt like the sort of book that I hoped to someday write. I don't think I've come close to that, but mine has pictures!"

—MATT DIFFEE, *New Yorker* cartoonist, author of *Hand Drawn Jokes for Smart Attractive People*

29. "Back in 1996, I got a job with Lands' End in Dodgeville. It's also how I met Garrison Keillor. A lot of the 'creatives' being copywriters, art directors, lived in Madison, but we decided to buy a house in Dodgeville, a very small farm town of about two thousand or so. The house we bought was small, all brick, but very eclectic. The woman who lived there also owned a bookstore, in Dubuque, Iowa, I think. She had closed her bookstore and sold out her entire inventory to Roseanne Barr and Tom Arnold, who were building some giant house in Iowa and just bought, like, thousands of books to fill it up and create the air of a learned, well-read couple with one fell swoop of a pen to a check. The ironic bit was I think they broke up before they ever lived in the house, which was so large that no private party would buy it, and it became like a public space, maybe a senior center or something like that. I have no idea what happened to all those books."

—MICHAEL SHAW, *New Yorker* cartoonist

---

30. Before Lauren Baratz-Logsted decided to be a writer she started working at Klein's of Westport, Connecticut. "The staff was encouraged to take books home to read, which would no doubt have horrified some of our customers were they ever to learn that they purchased preread books. But how else would we know to tell them whether a book lived up to the reviews? And there was no way I could support my five-book-a-week habit on my retail starter's salary. In many ways Klein's was a revelation, providing a far

more thorough and sweeping education than I'd received at any school. There was the day a woman came in with dark glasses on, tears streaming out from underneath. 'Just give me a good book.' She needed a book that could talk her off the ledge. So I gave her Olive Ann Burns's Cold Sassy Tree. I didn't try to describe it, I simply put it in her hands. A week later she returned without the dark glasses. 'Thank you for saving my life,' she said; then she proceeded to tell me all that had happened to her. All I can say is, it was a lot."

---

31. "New Yorker Books was known as an anti-war bookstore. We were on Broadway near Eighty-Ninth Street above the New Yorker Theater. One day, the police came by the store for selling Robert Crumb's Zap #4 because it included incest . . . the mother was with the son . . . or wait, was [it] that [the] father was with the son? . . . or the daughter . . . or everyone was with everyone or something like that . . . I'm not sure. Anyway they came to arrest someone, so they took our clerk, a Vietnam vet. [In 1969, Crumb's Joe Blow resulted in a number of obscenity arrests in New York City and elsewhere.] So wouldn't you know it, Gotham Book Mart organized a protest and rally to try to help us free our clerk. We tried to get R. Crumb to appear but he insisted he was not political."

—WARREN MILLER, onetime bookstore owner and renown *New Yorker* cartoonist

---

32. "When I first began writing and published my first book, the little store The Bookworm, in Katonah, New York, put it in the window. I didn't know they even knew who I was, but they did. After that it was in the window for a long time, and when my writing was going badly I used to walk past the window to look at it so that I could see that I did truly exist in the world."

—ROXANA ROBINSON, author of *Sparta*

---

33. "There is a great bookstore in Buenos Aires that carries mostly English-language books, and is sort of a home base for expats in Argentina. A few years ago I was there and bought some very interesting Spanish-to-English translations, including an illuminating side-by-side translation of one of Kate Chopin's stories. And I also got a guide to Spanish verbs, and inside this book, a used book, there was a single sheet of paper left there from the book's previous owner. The paper had the USAID logo at the top, and there were a bunch of telling notes written on the page, demonstrating the concerns and priorities of this particular USAID staffer."

—DAVE EGGERS

---

34. "It was January 1971 and my very first published picture book, Yellow Yellow, had just been released. The story was written by my Cooper Union classmate Frank Asch, and I had done the illustrations. I was with my friend Dimitri, and we went into the

Doubleday bookstore on Fifth Avenue and Fifty-Sixth Street to see if they had the book. Anyhow, there it was, prominently displayed on the wall! We took down a copy and looked through it. I was thrilled. Then Dimitri happened to look up at a bearded man standing nearby. 'You're a famous person,' said Dimitri, who was not at all shy and introduced himself, then me, then my book. The man was Jim Henson. He looked through Yellow Yellow and liked it a lot and decided to buy it. He gave me his card and said, 'Keep in touch,' which I did. Every time I had a new book published, I would send Jim Henson a copy. So, as far as I know, his kids grew up with my books. I did visit him one time up at the building where the Muppets were created. Very nice guy."

—MARK ALAN STAMATY, author of *Who Needs Donuts?*

---

35. "Some years back, John [Scioli] was very good about stocking my (two) books, and one day, walking by on Court Street, I was pleased to see that one of them was prominently displayed in the front window of Community Bookstore. As the days and weeks passed, however, I noticed that the front cover (it was a paperback) was—due to heat, humidity, sun, and John's ever-present cigarette smoke—slowly but surely curling back on itself. Finally, the cover was horribly curled all the way open and looked ghastly. Plus, you couldn't tell what the book was, which maybe was a blessing. I had hoped that John would take notice—how could he not?—and rectify the situation. But he never did. Finally, one day I entered the dark smoky store. Books and magazines and ephemera were stacked so high on the front counter that all I could see of John was the top of his head. 'John,' I said, 'Do you think maybe you could replace my book in the window with a new copy, one where the front cover isn't all curled open?' I see the top of his head rotate toward the window. An Everest of books, record albums, and (for some reason) children's toys were between him and the window. 'I would if I could,' he said, and that was that."

—NICK DOWNES, cartoonist

---

36. "I hang all the celebrity things like a letter from Jackie O. and pictures I've taken with Maureen Stapleton and Paul Newman up in the bathroom. One day I hear a patron exiting the bathroom. 'Boy, I never expected to see my picture over your toilet,' said a laughing James Taylor."

—MATTHEW TANNENBAUM, owner of The Bookstore

---

37. "There's also the time I went to Powell's on acid to buy an Allen Ginsburg book of poetry. We should talk."

—KURT OPPRECHT, writer

---

38. Harvard Book Store was the setting for a unique photo shoot. Novelist and grandniece of Sigmund Freud, Anne Bernays, and her husband, Pulitzer Prize winner Justin Kaplan, got a call from Cambridge Community Access Television: "Would we pose for a nude calendar? They were trying to get a lot of notable people in Cambridge. She promised it would be done 'tastefully.' . . . They opened early at seven o'clock on a Sunday morning to avoid gawkers and shot four or five rolls for maybe an hour and a half. . . . It was by far the most embarrassing photo shoot I'd ever taken part in, and if I had the chance to do it over, I probably would."

---

39. "I started taking my daughter to bookstores before she could walk. Every week and sometimes more than that, we'd go off to a bookstore. We'd spend hours in the kids' section, me reading to her until she began to read to me. As she grew, we'd go in and divide and conquer. I always told her to pick any book she'd like and I would get it for her if she read it. The times reading, talking books and life, is something that could not be paid for at any price. Watching my daughter learn to love reading and words is about all a dad could ask for in terms of education. She is now in college, but over breaks just to catch up we meet at a bookstore. While I have made my share of mistakes as a father, I'd have to rank the bookstore journeys as one success I will always treasure, and I hope that my daughter would say the same thing."

—A LOVING FATHER

ACKNOWLEDGMENTS

First I want to thank *New Yorker* editor Michael Agger, who gave me the assignment that this book is based on. Thank you, Michael, and I look forward to future projects together.

To my editor, Jay Sacher, who acquired and championed this book. It was a pleasure creating this book with you. Thank you also to designer Danielle Deschenes for your expertise and inspired packaging. I want to thank everyone at Penguin Random House who helped us, including Candice Chaplin, Kevin Sweeting, Natasha Martin, and Danielle Daitch.

Thank you to Garrison Keillor for your large contribution to the book and for years of inspiration. You set the bar for storytelling.

I had a lot of help from friends and met so many wonderful people during this project. Thank you to old and new friends for your support, sharing your stories, and introducing me to your favorite bookstores: Ellen S. Abramowitz, Wayne Alfano, Jonathan Ames, Frank Michael Angelo, Ilene Antelman, Catherine Arnold, Lesley Arrowsmith, Alec Baldwin, John Ballantine, Lauren Baratz-Logsted, Dave Barry, Todd Barry, Anne Bernays, Harry Bliss, David Borchart, Leslie Brada, Jan Brandt, Michal Brat, Louise Braverman, Kelly Brouse, Calef Brown, Pat Byrnes, Jen Campbell, Lou Carlozo, John Chandler, Con Chapman, Roz Chast, David Cheezem, Tracy Chevalier, Deepak Chopra, Ian Cochran, Amity Condie, Tobias Cox, Molly Crabapple, Heather Crothall, Aline & Robert Crumb, Elaine Dannemiller, Jon Delheim, Ann Dermansky, Dana DeVito, Christine DiCrocco, Matthew Diffee, Chris Doeblin, Liza Donnelly, Nick Downes, Jonathan Drucker, Heather Duncan, Jennifer Egan, Dave Eggers, David Enyeart, Rebecca Fitting, Joe Frank, Michal Frank, Leon Freilich, Donna Friedman, Drew Friedman, Neil Gaiman, Marianne Garnier, Richard Gere, Amitav Ghosh, Gary Gianni, Thomas Gianni, Dorothy Globus, Ken Gloss, Stewart "Adam Ant" Goddard, Peter Goff, Sharon Gold, Loren Goodman, Michelle Gross, Sam Gross, Terry Gross, David Grove, David Hackett, Amy Halloran, Fred Harper, Sid Harris, Jenny Hart, Amanda Hass, Ethan Hawke, Karen Hayes, Simon Heafield, Annie Hedrick, Sarah

Henshaw, Jan Herman, Ed Hermance, Jennifer Hixon, Carter B. Horsley, Eowyn Ivey, Rosemary James, Heather Johnson, Mark Kalinoski, Bruce Eric Kaplan, Mitchell Kaplan, Jacqueline Kellachan, John K. King, Charles Kochman, Susan Konar, Edward Koren, Rick Kotrba, Ken Krimstein, Christiaan Kuypers, Lea Lane, Leslie Lanier, Jean-Philippe Laroche, Raul Lemesoff, Jonathan Lethem, Arnie Levin, Stacey Lewis, Christopher Lione, Bob Mankoff, Marc Maron, Patricia Marx, Michael Maslin, Liz Mason, Jeffrey Mayersohn, Katherine Stebbins McCaffrey, Patti McCracken, Steve Meltzer, Prof. Ifeanyi Menkiti, Cheryl Mesler, Sharon Mesmer, Susan Mihalic, Cat Mihos, Andrew Miller, Warren Miller, Ivan Mistrik, Sonja Mistrik, Jay Moore, Jim Moore, Doris Moskowitz, Dolores Motichka, Matt Mueller, Arthur Murdock, Karen Murdock, Parke Muth, Vlad Niculescu, Cristina Nosti, Bob Odenkirk, Naomi Odenkirk, Karen Opas, Kurt Opprecht, Michael Palin, Teresa Burns Parkhurst, Nathaniel Philbrick, Joe Philips, Jenelle Pifer, Mary Ellen Piland, Greg Powers, Darryl Price, Jon Privett, Greg Proops, Shawn Purcell, Charla Puryear, Jordan Puryear, Bill Reed, Prof. Michael Reichling, Jake Reiss, Ari Rieser, David Remnick, Roxana Robinson, David S. Rose, Gil Roth, Davy Rothbart, Lee Runchey, Tiffany Sainz, Donna Sandstrom, Jennifer Scanlan, Charles J. Shields, Christine Shields, Tina Simms, Lenore Skenazy, Esther K. Smith, Judi Smith, Scott Snibbe, Gary Sohmers, Em-J Staples, Hillel Stavis, Alan Steinfeld, Colin Stokes, Martin Stokes, Allen Stone, Julia Suits, Kim Sutton, Nialle Sylvan, Susan Takacs, Matthew Tannenbaum, Anthony Tao, Eric Thornton, Lynne Tillman, Tom Toro, Britton Trice, Kelly Van Valkenburg, Emily Vizzo, Bart Vlek, Joe Vonnegut, Carol Wald, Jessica Walker, Chris Ware, Prof. Henry Weinfield, Marcia Wernick, Sylvia Whitman, Sean Wilentz, Mo Willems, Morris Witten, Ben Wolf, Barbara Yeaman, Michael Allen Zell, Ursula Cary Ziemba, Lisa Zucker . . . and Mike Sacks, who helped personally and whose books *Poking a Dead Frog* and *And Here's the Kicker* provided direction.

Additionally I want to give special thanks to the following, without whom there is no book:

To poet/writer Ron Kolm, who knows more about the bookstore scene than anyone I met, generously gave me much of his time, and is a really talented, nice guy.